MERAKI

JYOTIRMOY MANIAR

Chennai • Bangalore

CLEVER FOX PUBLISHING
Chennai, India

Published by CLEVER FOX PUBLISHING 2025
Copyright © Jyotirmoy Maniar 2025

All Rights Reserved.
ISBN: 978-93-67074-68-8

This book has been published with all reasonable efforts taken to make the material error-free after the consent of the author. No part of this book shall be used, reproduced in any manner whatsoever without written permission from the author, except in the case of brief quotations embodied in critical articles and reviews.

The Author of this book is solely responsible and liable for its content including but not limited to the views, representations, descriptions, statements, information, opinions and references ["Content"]. The Content of this book shall not constitute or be construed or deemed to reflect the opinion or expression of the Publisher or Editor. Neither the Publisher nor Editor endorse or approve the Content of this book or guarantee the reliability, accuracy or completeness of the Content published herein and do not make any representations or warranties of any kind, express or implied, including but not limited to the implied warranties of merchantability, fitness for a particular purpose. The Publisher and Editor shall not be liable whatsoever for any errors, omissions, whether such errors or omissions result from negligence, accident, or any other cause or claims for loss or damages of any kind, including without limitation, indirect or consequential loss or damage arising out of use, inability to use, or about the reliability, accuracy or sufficiency of the information contained in this book.

Cover and Doodle Designs by Manasi Khandpekar (Manache)
Email: manacheinc@gmail.com

BORN TO BE REAL, NOT PERFECT...

Life is a collection of moments—some small, some large—that together shape who we are. This book is a journey through those moments, drawn from the pages of everyday life, filled with laughter, lessons, and love. Inspired by the people I've met, the places I've been, and the experiences that have colored my world, I invite you to take a walk through my stories.

What has motivated me to write is the desire to share these moments—those fleeting yet profound snapshots of life—that have shaped me and continue to inspire me. Writing became a way to capture the beauty, the humor, and the lessons in a world that often moves too quickly to pause and reflect. Inspired by the desire to pour my soul into something meaningful, *Meraki* became a reflection of passion, creativity, and the love I've found in life's simplest moments.

As we go through the highs and lows, the funny and the heartfelt, I hope you find a piece of yourself in these pages. Whether it's a familiar memory, a laugh shared, or a thought that sparks something new, my wish is for these words to create a connection between us—one that feels both personal and universal.

So, grab a cup of coffee, make yourself comfortable, and let's embark on this journey together. The road ahead is full of surprises, and I'm excited to share it with you, one story at a time.

For my parents Smt. & Shri Chary
my spouse Sameer
& my daughter Priyal

CONTENTS

1. 'Celebrate Life' No Matter What 1
2. Being A Lifelong Learner 7
3. Humbling Resilience 15
4. Passion For Creativity 21
5. Faith Is The Answer 29
6. My Superpowers 35
7. An Unconditional Support 43
8. How People Shape You 51
9. The Phoenix Within 57
10. The Joy Of Giving 65
11. Friendships As I Know It 71
12. Work-Life Integration 77
13. Spirituality Is A Strength 83
14. Wonders Of Travelling 89
15. No Pain No Gain 97
16. Nurturing Happiness 105
17. A Writer's Journey 112
18. A Letter To My Younger Self 115

"A father is neither an anchor to hold us back nor a sail to take us there, but a guiding light whose love shows us the way."

CHAPTER 1

'CELEBRATE LIFE' NO MATTER WHAT

*T*his first story carries an incredible lesson learned from my dad which has been the guiding light of my life. The lesson has shaped me, my behavior, personality, relationships, career, and life. I cannot thank my dad enough for teaching me this lesson during one of the toughest times of our lives. No one could ever know what he was going through, but all he wanted for me was to live my life with one thought – 'Celebrate Life' no matter what.

This story goes back to my teenage years. It is a memory which I have cherished close to my heart despite it being a tragic one. It is said that difficult times teach and shape you for the better.

It was one of my teenage birthdays. Any teenager would be absolutely excited and plan her birthday in the most pompous way. But I was in no mood to celebrate as my dad was fighting the toughest battle of his life for one year then. We knew we were going to lose him, yet our hope and his health condition made it all so painful and uncertain.

It was he who insisted that everyone celebrate my birthday. My close friends were invited home to stay. We celebrated in the simplest way possible. We sat chatting all through the night. Meanwhile, my dad vomited blood in the next room. But neither did my mom, who was with him the entire night, nor my dad tell us about it.

The next morning, he was admitted to the hospital, to never came back home alive. In his deteriorating condition, all he wanted was for his daughter to celebrate every moment of her life.

All our lives changed completely. Nothing was ever the same.

All of a sudden, I was forced to grow up. The grief can never be completely gone. Things were hard, but we took it all in our stride and continued to live the last lesson he taught us - 'Celebrate Life' no matter what.

My dad was born in a humble joint family with many siblings, cousins and relatives all living together. Financially, they belonged to a modest income level. Right from childhood, there were two striking characteristics he displayed— big aspirations for the family and relentless hard work.

As a kid he would sit under a streetlight to study. He would also motivate his friends coming from affluent families to join him for studies. He would teach and inspire them to pursue their own goals. Even today, all his friends are connected to our family, and share stories about his inspiring personality with pride.

Being humble and living a life of gratitude is one of the many qualities that come to me naturally, thanks to my dad. I remember one incident that happened during my summer internship at a reputable CA firm. I had to collate all audit reports and was paid a small stipend in return. During that time, I received a small bonus amount and some sweets from the company. I used the amount to buy a bag and a shirt for my dad, a saree for my mom and a T-shirt for my brother. It made me feel so proud.

But what made it all so special was a handwritten note that my dad wrote to the company thanking them for the sweets they sent home and the bonus they gave me. He mentioned his gratitude to them for taking care of his daughter. It was quite a legacy kind of company, and they all were sweetly astounded by his humble act of gratitude. They were all in awe of receiving a hand-written thank you note. In similar ways, he would always go out of his way to make people feel genuinely appreciated.

He believed in creating a nurturing and supportive environment where each member felt valued and loved. This foundation of care and responsibility shaped not only his life but also the lives of those around him. His dedication was a beacon of warmth and security, ensuring that his family never felt the strains of uncertainty despite our frequent relocations due to transfers in his job.

Starting humbly as a clerk and gradually working his way up to one of the most senior positions, earning immense respect from everyone in the bank, was all due to his aspiration, valuable contributions, and uncompromising hard work, day in and day out.

His journey was more than just a career; it was a testament to the power of perseverance and the importance of prioritizing loved ones. He taught us that true success is not measured by personal accolades but by the happiness and well-being of those we hold dear. His legacy is one of love, sacrifice, and boundless support, a legacy that continues to inspire us to this day.

On the day he passed away, a big crowd had gathered at the hospital to pay him respect and console us. The doctors were amazed and enquired more about his background, thinking he might be a famous personality, like a politician. However, the crowd gathered there consisted of people who were genuinely touched by his care, love, and support. As the saying goes, "People may not remember your status or wealth, but they do remember how you made them feel." This was proven true that day, when each one person present there had a sincere reason to be there, whether it was his inspiring words, heartfelt appreciation, earnest support, or the beautiful feelings he left with them.

He is still remembered for his courteous nature at the bank where he worked. He always put everyone else ahead of himself—first his family, then his friends, followed by colleagues and associates at work, and countless others he encountered throughout his life. Interestingly, the only argument that I ever heard from mom against him was that he never ever thought about himself. I remember people would often come to our home, either to converse or to simply listen to him. His words made great impact on many people's lives that we, his family, had no idea about it. But we got to know many such stories after he expired.

It's been years since he left this world, but his friends have always stayed connected with us. They genuinely helped us during the tough times to get back on our feet. To this day, they regularly check in on us, always wishing us well.

Life was never easy. We needed to fight our own battles, make decisions, and sail together through the ups and downs of life.

Through his actions, Dad instilled in us the values of hard work, empathy, and the joy of giving. We learned that family is not just an important thing, it's everything. His life was a beautiful tapestry woven with threads of devotion and selflessness, reminding us of the profound impact one person can have through acts of love and kindness.

Reflecting on my journey today, balancing the roles of daughter, wife, and mother fills my heart with pride. The path from being an executive assistant to leading a team and making a lasting impact has been deeply rewarding. But above all, the greatest triumph is embracing my father's legacy of celebrating life in all its forms, no matter the obstacles.

My Dad, My Hero
Late Shri T. V. L. N. Chary

Little me with my mom & dad

"Anyone who stops learning is old whether at twenty or eighty. Anyone who keeps learning stays young."

– Henry Ford.

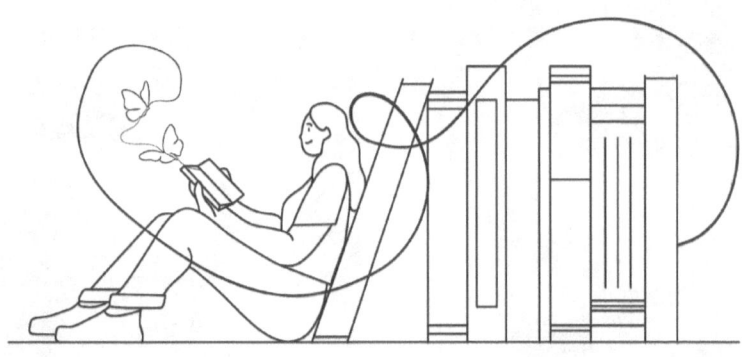

CHAPTER 2

BEING A LIFELONG LEARNER

$\mathcal{M}$y father, owing to his hard work, dedication, and learning attitude, coupled with his aspirations grew to the senior most position in the bank. As per the bank rules, he was transferred to new locations, and the entire family had to keep moving from place to place.

Family was always at the heart of his life. His first and foremost thought in every decision was, 'How will this benefit my family? Will it bring them comfort?' His greatest aspiration was to give his family the best life possible, and it was this deep devotion that fueled his tireless work ethic, driving him to rise through the ranks and secure a brighter future for them.

We all observed his genuine and dedicated efforts to progress in his banking career. With each promotion, the family was going to enjoy financial benefits and additional perks. Achieving the next position would provide greater comfort for his family. Therefore, he consistently worked hard and sought to expand his knowledge, striving diligently to earn that promotion.

His selflessness could be easily seen in each of his decisions and actions. As simple as bringing the snacks received at any office celebrations back home. He would never relish those snacks alone in the office. Instead, he would prefer to see us enjoying them in the comfort of our home. He would never indulge in luxuries for himself, yet he happily invested significant amounts in valuable comforts for his children.

Among the numerous lessons I have learned from him, the principle of 'Keep Learning to Grow' is one I observed him embody throughout his life. I believe my mother also drew her inspiration to continue learning from him. When life took a significant turn and she needed to enter the workforce, she embraced the challenge and worked hard to advance in her career. This concept, whether intentional or not, was ingrained in my mind from a young age by the two strongest influences in my life.

In college, I was driven by my ambition to grow. But with my father's death, I had to look for jobs while graduating. I applied for two vacant positions in a multinational organization. One was an Executive Assistant, and the other was an Assistant in the Distribution department. Out of 22 candidates, 2 of us were shortlisted. I secretly prayed that I wouldn't be offered the role of Executive Assistant. I was ready to learn everything about the Distribution process and work, but I did not wish to take on a secretarial position. There was a funny reason for that as well–the bollywood movies I had watched till then gave me a stupid impression that every secretary has an affair with her boss. It may sound hilarious now, but at that age, it was a scary thought.

Well, life had other plans for me. I was presented with a position of Executive Assistant that I had desperately hoped to avoid, yet I had no choice but to take it on. I embraced this challenge with the determination to excel and work diligently to advance in my career. Rather than complaining about my role as a secretary, I focused on continuous learning and consistently delivered my work with excellence. I made it a priority to acquire as much knowledge as I could.

In my role as a secretary, I observed the preferential treatment that every senior executive arriving from the Mumbai head office received. Interactions with my seniors always amazed me with their knowledge and their power to lead teams. They also inspired me to 'Think Big.' Be it the aspiration to grow on a daily basis or the urge to give the best to my family just like my parents, it all kept driving me towards excellence.

Advancing in a career required higher qualifications. Taking a break from my job for higher studies was not my first choice. Hence, I decided to pursue a night Management Degree. People and Human Resources as a subject intrigued me. I discovered a reputable management college in Mumbai, NMIMS, that offered an appropriate management course in HR. Since it was a night college, and I was married with a child, I initially felt skeptical about attending the classes. Thoughts about my peers, how people would react, and how I would manage everything filled my mind with doubt. But as I started, I realized there were many other people just like me who had bigger aspirations and were on a similar path.

Pursuing a management Course while working demanded immense effort, discipline, and dedication on my part. Balancing a full-time job and a family with night classes required me to meticulously plan my days and manage my time effectively. Often, my evenings were filled with lectures, assignments, and group projects, leaving little room for leisure and family time. Yet, the knowledge and skills I gained were invaluable, fueling my passion for growth and advancement in my career.

The journey had several challenges. Juggling responsibilities was overwhelming and would leave me exhausted. However, the immense support of my family, colleagues and also peers at college kept me motivated. We shared a mutual understanding of the sacrifices each of us was making, which fostered a sense of unity and encouragement.

I learned a lot of new concepts which unlocked new perspectives and opportunities. I eagerly applied the learning to my work projects and witnessed how education could enhance my professional capabilities. The overall experience, along with the challenges that I overcame, taught me flexibility and adaptability. These are the qualities that serve me well in my career.

Completing my management degree not only expanded my professional horizons but also instilled a deep sense of accomplishment. It reinforced my belief in the power of lifelong learning and the incredible potential within each of us to rise above challenges and achieve our dreams.

Along with the tangible benefits, I was also reaping some good intangible benefits. Earning my management degree significantly influenced how my colleagues and superiors perceived me. Staying relevant and updated with industry knowledge and information greatly enhanced my confidence when engaging with senior executives and it was evident in every conversation and presentation.

In concrete terms, I received the opportunity to take on more creative and innovative cross-functional and cross-regional projects that significantly benefited the company in the long run. Recognizing digital communications as the future, I pursued a postgraduate degree in Digital Marketing and Communications from Mudra Institute of Communications Ahmedabad (MICA). Thanks to my educational progress and enthusiastic involvement in innovative projects, I advanced to the various senior profiles within the organization. Being versatile, the long-held dream of moving beyond a secretary role was finally realized, bringing me an incredible sense of accomplishment.

Throughout the years, I have received numerous awards, and I take great pride in highlighting some of the most significant ones that have added a delightful touch to my journey. The Managing Director's Recognition Award, which I earned for consistently going the extra mile, stands out as my proudest achievement. Another noteworthy accolade is the Game Changer Award. Additionally, I must mention my first creative project, 'HUMTUM,' which gained recognition by securing a prominent feature in the organization's multinational magazine and allowed me to lead our champion team in Paris with great pride.

Lifelong learning has been the cornerstone of my growth and accomplishments. Looking ahead, I am passionate about making a positive impact on people's lives. I strive to add a personal touch with empathy, helping to make life easier and more beautiful for others. This passion inspired me to pursue a certificate program in Leadership Principles through Harvard Business School Online and also engaged with International Coach Federation to be certified as a Coach.

However, my reflections on these specific programs will be shared in another chapter of this book. One thing is certain: my commitment to lifelong learning has only deepened with time, and I intend to continue this journey of growth. That is a promise I make to myself.

This chapter of my life serves as a testament to the belief that with determination and perseverance, anything is achievable.

"Always walk through life as if you have something new to learn and you will."

– Vermon Howard.

KEY INSIGHTS

- Education is just one form of learning; keep exploring beyond getting a degree.

- Continuously learn and grow in areas that spark your interest.

- Take tough decisions, even when they seem impossible.

- Hard work is essential for growth and success.

- Lifelong learning enhances your sense of fulfillment and purpose.

- Small, consistent steps are more valuable than big, inconsistent decisions.

"A mother's resilience is like a tree in a storm, bending but never breaking."

CHAPTER 3

HUMBLING RESILIENCE

*T*his is the story of a young woman who fought through the biggest crisis of her life by transforming her own self from a dependent housewife to an independent and self-empowered mother.

"Being challenged in life is inevitable. Being defeated is optional." She was challenged from all sides in life, but defeat was not possible as she rose to shine from within through her courage and empathy. It is rightly said, "Rise above the storm and you will find the sunshine."

Like my dad, my mom grew up in a humble, modest home with many siblings. My grandparents were quite disciplined and strict, especially my grandfather. He was very particular about daily routines and strictly ensured everything at home happened at a specific time.

My mother embraced these qualities and continues to live by them to this day. She truly embodies the legacy of discipline and meticulousness at her core. Anytime you visit her, the home is spic and span, she is neatly dressed, and her behavior absolutely prim and proper. At her current age, she maintains a proper diet and time management even on holidays. Like us, there are no cheat days or cheat meals in her dictionary. She duly follows the rulebook of the good life.

One more thing that she is very strict about is her daily prayers and rituals. She says, "My God is watching and he will take care of everything." Her staunch belief in God has given her great strength all through her life.

My mom married very early. At an age when we usually attend college, she became a mom to me. Her entire life circled around her home and family, which was my dad, my little brother and myself. As you know, my dad was a government employee who rose to a senior position in the bank over the years and we all enjoyed the luxuries and perks. Residing at a prime location in Mumbai provided as a perk by the bank, we always had help available for even the smallest of work, for example, even to change the light bulbs, curtains etc.

While delightfully living a secure life of 35 years, my mom had to face life's biggest crisis— losing her husband, the backbone of our family. For us kids, we lost our father, but for my mom, she lost the light of her day, the quiet of her night, and the hope of her life. Her loss cannot be put into words. Feelings of anxiety, guilt, fear, instability— she went through it all. But looking at her children, a teenage daughter and a young son, she had to push all her struggles aside and rise to make crucial decisions in life.

The first decision was to move from our bank-provided home in Mumbai to Hyderabad. Life had to be rebuilt from scratch. From relocating to setting up new gas and phone connections, and arranging all the essentials of home and life, she had to handle everything on her own. Unlike before, there was no assistance available. Additionally, we noticed people's perspectives changing, with some expressing thoughts and concerns that initially upset my mom a great deal.

The bank offered a compensation clerical job at a very junior level. We pushed our mom to accept it. For a homebound, undergraduate woman, it was a big decision.. She showed amazing courage to accept and work under bosses who were very junior to her husband. She completed her graduation online through an Open University and enrolled in additional courses to upgrade herself.

From setting up a new home, dealing with changed perspectives, and upgrading herself, to going to work every day and facing the challenges of a government job, she handled it all. She fought the discomfort of working under her husband's juniors, raised a daughter and son, educated and settled them, and went out of her way to assist customers at the bank branch, making them feel comfortable. She did all of this single-handedly while managing her internal struggles.

Starting as a junior clerk, she went on to retire after two decades, earning recognition for Best Customer Service. She became the most sought-after executive, with customers waiting for her to resolve their issues. Over time, she built a strong reputation and an identity for herself

She had a fixed routine during her job which got disrupted after her retirement and made her anxious. But as time passed, she fetched her own ways to keep herself busy. It was gratifying to see her using her time constructively. Seeing my dad suffering in the last days, she was always extra cautious about her diet and health.

We kids are thankful for her disciplined nature, which keeps her healthy and independent. And funnily, we try our best to avoid being lazy and careless in front of her even today.

From being completely dependent on her spouse for both small and significant milestones in life to becoming independent and ensuring that every little need for her children was met, she carved out a life of ease and comfort through immense effort.

From being an anxious, depressed young widow to becoming a role model of courage, self-motivation, and empowerment, she encouraged my brother and me to build independent lives for ourselves. She exhibited the true meaning and power of independence to us.

One thing which has never left her is her empathy. She always gave us the lesson, "Empathize with others, keeping aside one's problems," and she is a living example of this lesson.

I have encountered numerous feminists who talk volumes on feminism and related topics. However, my mother embodies the true essence of feminism for me. Her ability to balance nurturing her family while building her own place in society is a testament to her strength and resilience. She has taught me that being a feminist means standing up for one's rights, supporting others, and embracing one's individuality without hesitation or apology.

For everyone, their mom is the most special person in life. For me, she is more than special. She is my role model, my hero.

"**Liberty, when it begins to take root, is a plant of rapid growth.**" *Dil se...* I thank my mom for having built the ambition in me to be an independent and self-empowered woman.

My Mom, My Inspiration
Smt. Radha Chary

With my mom & brother

Mom & Dad

"One day you will look back and see that all along you were blooming."

CHAPTER 4
PASSION FOR CREATIVITY

*I*n the corporate world, some tricky situations need a unique solution. It's these moments that truly test our creativity and adaptability. Without wanting to sound pompous, most of the time I have come up with out-of-the-box solutions along with my teams. Further, I have been asked "Jyoti, how do you manage to come up with such unique ideas?" I would just shrug.

Now that I sit back and think about these questions, I guess the answer lies back in my childhood days, when my creativity was nurtured and blossomed under the loving guidance of my parents.

"Every child is an artist." My parents were one of the ardent believers of this quote.

My mom believed that girls learning creative arts added value to their personality. And she was absolutely against wasting time. She would stress so much upon making the best and wisest use of time. Hence, Art and Time were two great motivations for my mom to enroll me in a new hobby class every summer vacation.

Over my childhood years, getting an extra push for all co-curricular activities, I have been introduced to and mastered many creative pursuits. From knitting, fabric painting, making teddy bears, greeting cards, and rangolis, to saree draping, these pursuits unknowingly created lasting impressions on my mind, choices and personality as well.

I am also trained in classical Veena, vocal singing and Bharatnatyam. I would perform on stage in many shows, thus developing a deep appreciation for cultural heritage and instilling confidence in me to express myself creatively.

My dad was very devotional and wished me to incorporate spirituality into my life. Every Sunday morning, he would make me sit on his scooter and ride to Ramakrishna Math in Hyderabad, a beautiful serene place which housed a library with many books, a temple and various activities for students.

An 82-year-old lady would teach the Bhagwad Geeta to kids. She would emphasize that the 11th & 15th Chapters had the power to cleanse you from within by its recitation. For two hours every Sunday, I would be a sincere student trying to impress my dad. Who knew what my real motivation was? Well, there's no harm in sharing this now after all these years. If you're familiar with South Indian homes, you'd know that biscuits are rarely found in them, and my home was no exception. However, after sitting through her class for two hours, we were given either two Parle-G biscuits or two Marie biscuits. For a young child, biscuits were far more motivating than spirituality.

Whatever the motivation, I am glad my father took me there every Sunday religiously. And I made a sincere effort to learn. And above that, my teacher was fond of me and took a special interest in me since I was trained in classical singing. All of this learning landed me the shiny first prize for the Bhagwad Geeta recitation in an interschool competition in Hyderabad! That made me feel extremely proud of myself in front of my entire school and my parents as well.

My father was very proud of me. He would make me recite the Bhagwad Geeta on every auspicious occasion. His happiness knew no bounds seeing his little girl walking on the spiritual path. I vividly remember, before slipping into coma, he asked me to recite the Bhagwad Geeta for him. Closing his eyes, he clenched my hand till I finished the recitation. I never saw him conscious again after that moment, and those last moments with him hold a very special place in my heart.

As a child, when I was pushed to spend my time wisely by attending all the hobby classes, I never understood the importance of it. Now, I do believe that parents make super extra efforts, and these efforts influence and mould a child's future thinking and personality for the better. On the surface, you may be learning a hobby. But deep inside, there are so many intangible skills getting developed.

These childhood pursuits made creativity an integral part of my personality. In turn, my creative passion has helped me in several ways - multitasking, finding creative solutions, improving my problem-solving ability, enhancing my interpersonal relationships, boosting empathic behavior, broadening perspectives, and so much more. Interacting with so many hobby teachers and peers has also given me a knack for understanding people from different walks of life.

Moreover, this passion for creativity has given me a great competitive edge in my career graph. I could have comfortably stayed in the secretarial position. However, wanting to exercise this passion for creativity kept my mind open to opportunities. And when these opportunities came knocking on the door, I was ready to welcome them with open arms.

A simple newsletter was to be made for the company's rural sales force. Taking some motivating stories from different departments and collating them together with some knowledge sharing, how creative could it get? Yet, I saw an opportunity to infuse creativity into this task and make it truly impactful. Instead of a standard newsletter, I envisioned a vibrant, engaging piece that not only shared stories but also uplifted and inspired our rural sales force.

To begin with, I needed a name which would be simple but catchy and can linger in the minds of people. I was introduced by a colleague to Manasi, a passionate professional Graphic Designer. Little did I know that this professional encounter with her would later turn into a lifelong friendship. We share an amazing rapport when it comes to work right from that first call till date. And our friendship stands on mutual understanding, trust and love for creativity.

With her support, we went through and rejected many names for their mundane nature. Then, 'HUM TUM' caught our attention. Once that was finalized, we created a beautiful logo and tagline: 'Kuch tum bolo, kuch hum bole.' I decided that in every issue, we would feature stories from both the head office and the sales force.

I began by weaving personal anecdotes and success stories from various departments, highlighting the incredible achievements and contributions of individuals often working behind the scenes. Each story was paired with motivational quotes and practical tips, creating a tapestry of inspiration and learning.

To make the newsletter visually appealing and interesting, Manasi suggested the idea of comic strips. Together, we incorporated colorful illustrations and infographics that simplified complex ideas and made the content more accessible. Interactive elements, like quizzes and feedback sections, were included to encourage reader participation and foster a sense of community.

The result was more than just a newsletter; it was a catalyst for connection and motivation, reminding our rural sales force of their vital role in the company's success. This creative endeavor not only served its purpose but also reinforced my belief that even the simplest tasks can be transformed into meaningful experiences through creativity and thoughtful execution.

HUM TUM gained great momentum and recognition from all levels of the company. While the sales force would eagerly wait for the next issue, people from different departments wanted to become a part of the newsletter and enthusiastically shared their stories.

It had a great impact on my career as I became a well-known face in the entire company. Even the Managing Director travelled to launch the inaugural issue. It was an unexpected honor that truly marked a turning point in my professional journey.

Furthermore, after the release of a few more issues of HUM TUM, he personally met me to appreciate the impact of the 'HUM TUM' newsletter and expressed a keen interest in fostering more innovative projects that could unite and motivate our workforce. Sitting across the Managing Director, I felt a deep sense of gratitude and excitement. It also gave me an opportunity to share my ideas and aspirations, and to learn from a leader whose experience and wisdom were both inspiring and enlightening.

This meeting reinforced my belief in the power of creativity and the value of taking initiative. It highlighted the importance of stepping out of comfort zones and embracing new challenges with enthusiasm and determination.

Reflecting on this experience, I realized that every creative endeavor, no matter how small it seems, can lead to significant opportunities and personal growth. Further, I was entrusted with many such opportunities to create impactful creative communications for the company.

Along with HUM TUM, I was also involved in creating diverse initiatives through caricatures like Khabarilal & Topilal. These initiatives mainly focused on sharing competitive information and enabling the rural field force in communication skills.

And, of course, how can I not mention the golden opportunity of getting featured in the International Innovative Project Repository. It was circulated in the Managing Director Conclave which had a participants from over 72 countries.

My creative pursuits have stimulated me to earn many rewards and recognitions in my career. Furthermore, it has made me grow in my career and be a positive contributor throughout my journey.

I read this quote somewhere, "Creativity is your superpower. Use it to change the world." And yes, I have and am experiencing it through my own life.

My first ever Brand Creatives

"You don't get to choose your brother. He is God's gift to you."

CHAPTER 5
FAITH IS THE ANSWER

*B*rothers are those naughty boys of the family who suddenly transform into a man in challenging times. The transition from boy to man is so smooth, unnoticed, and natural that we often wonder, 'Was he always like this, or were we mistaken in our understanding of him?' I have been a close witness to this transformation.

Like any other siblings, our childhood story began with his mischief, my fighting back, sibling rivalry, him taking the blame on my behalf, us fighting and protecting each other, and so on. It followed the textbook of childhood and sibling relationships. But always, in the back of my mind, there was a sense of peace knowing he would always be there to take care of me.

I recall a classic sibling tale that's quite funny. A childhood escapade where my brother donned the superhero cape of "Always Got Your Back." Picture this: our parents had to travel, leaving us at Auntie's place for a few days. I saw her making up delicious Gulab Jamuns for my birthday! Temptation was too strong, so at the night hour, I tiptoed into the kitchen.

With those sweet Gulab Jamuns in front of me, I thought, "Let's eat a few. No one's counting!" And just like that, I started with two or three… and then two or three more… and more! They were so delicious that I just couldn't stop until I had finished off half the container! Oops! I quickly kept it back in its spot.

The next morning, I played the innocent card like a pro and threw all the blame on my little bro. By the way, I looked sweet and innocent as a child, and I took utmost advantage of it. My poor brother took the heat from Auntie without a complaint. He knew it was me but still took the blame like a champ. What a boy! To this day, he's still my go-to scapegoat, ready to take the fall for his sister. I do feel a bit guilty, but oh, how loved I feel when he dotes on me and checks in on every little thing! That's the perfect brotherly love!

Right from childhood, my brother loved two things: Dancing and Cooking. Just like he would try out every new dance style, he would experiment with food in the kitchen too. Nothing else would make him happier than breaking into a dance step and cooking a yummy delicacy. These two passions have kept him going through life with enthusiasm.

Time and circumstances changed. My dad's death completely changed our lives. As we were coping with the loss of our family backbone, my younger brother who had transformed into the man of the family met with a major accident.

Always careful around the gas in the kitchen, one day he left the gas knob open while fetching the lighter. The next moment, there was an explosion, and the entire upper portion of his body was burned, including his eyelashes.

The visual memory hasn't faded away. One thing remained absolutely intact. It was the locket he wore on his neck. The locket with his most beloved– Hanuman. His faith in Hanuman was always a driving force in his life. His connection with his faith was very strong and nothing could take it away. This faith also built exceptional patience in him.

As we rushed him to the hospital, we were tormented but his faith kept our faith alive too. Over the next days, he went through continuous treatment and, of course, unbearable pain. Yet, he kept assuring us, "Don't worry. Have faith. Everything will be fine."

As the treatment went on, he still had to attempt the college 1st-year final exams by taking a proxy writer. It was an extreme struggle to talk yet he successfully managed to complete and pass the exams. What must have propelled him to go on in that stressful situation? Nothing but faith.

This faith in his deity and in his own self later took him to Mumbai for further studies. Well, the struggles weren't over yet. During his studies he was staying at a hostel. One day, while dancing he slipped so badly that his kneecap got dislocated. He struggled but fought it all with the support of his friends and showed a lot of grit.

More than love, I started respecting him for his faith and patience. But there was one incident that impacted me the most. Just two days before my marriage, I had to be hospitalized due to food poisoning. Due to unavoidable circumstances, the marriage couldn't be postponed. I was taken directly from the hospital to the wedding venue. And post the marriage ceremony I boarded the train along with my new family to my new home.

A new home, a new family, and new relationships awaited me, yet I didn't even know what was in my bag or what was missing. A bride typically packs her bag with utmost care, ensuring she can easily find her belongings in her new home. But I never got the chance, as I was in the hospital. My brother had to do it for me.

With great anxiety, I opened the bag on reaching my new home. And what did I see? To my great surprise, it was packed perfectly, just as I would have done it myself. A woman always thinks carefully and deeply while packing, considering how to arrange clothes based on occasions and including the essential personal items. Yet, my little brother had thought of everything, just as I would have. For a moment, I wondered if I was missing the memory of packing my own bag. How could he have done it so well? The memory of finding a perfectly packed bag has always stuck with me. More than perfection, my brother's thoughtfulness, foresightedness about my needs, and carefulness all became so evident to me in that one small incident.

From the little brother who took the blame for me to the one who meticulously packed my bag, to this day, I am absolutely in awe and feel blessed to have a brother who treats me like a princess. I have watched him grow beautifully in every role of his life—from a son to a brother, to a husband, and now to the father of a beautiful girl. In every role and every situation, one thing has remained constant: his leap of faith and his complete surrender to it.

As my younger brother, he has continued to display an array of lessons for me to grasp. Nothing needed to be said verbally; his actions spoke volumes. And I, though the elder one, have always and will always continue learning from him. One thing that is deeply engraved in me through him is this: "Don't worry. Have faith, and in the end, everything will work out." It is so true.

Every day of our life is not smooth. We face struggles one after the other. What helps is Faith which brings the power of patience, and keeps you strong through the challenges. Struggles and challenges will keep coming, and the only way to stand tall and fight through them is to keep faith that all will be okay.

"Keep the Faith. Hold on. It might be stormy now, but it can't rain forever." I thank my brother for this beautiful lesson.

With my lil champ, my brother, Satish

Satish & his Wife Gayatri

Satish with his little angel

"The best way to predict the future is to create it. You have the power within you to rise."

CHAPTER 6

MY SUPERPOWERS

$\mathcal{B}$eing a fresh graduate and stepping into a corporate office felt like being an amateur trekker standing at the foot of a massive mountain. I had no training for even simple hiking, no manual of do's and don'ts, and no guide, yet there I was, squinting to see the peak. Intimidated by the enormous challenge ahead, I also faced an internal mountain of doubts, skepticism, anxiety, and fear about confronting the obstacles before me.

My dad's journey of consistent growth and aspiration to do and give more each time stuck with me. This became my greatest motivation to dream big, do more, and achieve more in my life. As young dreamers, we often idolize the larger than life super heroes. But the truth is, the real superheroes are the everyday people around us—those who dare to think big and put in extraordinary effort to turn their dreams into reality. Thinking big is not only like winning a Nobel Prize but also winning over our own doubts and having courage to take necessary actions everyday.

I am happy and proud to share the lessons I've learned during the early years of my career. I call these my **Super Powers** because they have truly empowered me throughout my journey.

Super Power 1:
Dream Big

More than a decade ago, a coaching program was organised in our office. We were to choose our coaching partners from among our colleagues. When I sat down with my coach, I spoke about several things with a bit of hesitation at first. As we dwelled deeper, a question arose about the distant future. And in a flash, I replied, "I want to create a Brand for myself." It startled my partner, but then he came up with a series of detailed questions: What brand? What product or service? What is the market? What is the strategy? Communication, brand personality, brand identity, brand voice, competitors and so on.

I stared back at him, my mind blank. I had no clue about anything. I just wanted to create my own brand. I was dreaming big but had never taken the time to think it through. I wasn't even aware that such detailed planning was necessary for creating a brand. Over the years, that dream seemed to have taken a backseat as professional and personal responsibilities drove me forward. But a few years back, when I embarked on my journey as a professional life coach, the dream of creating a brand came to life.

I reconnected with my friend Manasi to help me design the brand and its communication strategy. She presented me with a detailed questionnaire, much like the one I had faced years ago. This time, however, I was prepared and did my homework thoroughly.

Finally, I created my brand – 'BE YOU'. As an individual and a certified coach , I have interacted with many people and listened to their stories. What struck me is that each individual is unique. I cannot be you, and you cannot be me. Hence, my focus of communication was clear: whatever you do… Be yourself.

While reflecting on my life stories to create the brand's message, another key theme emerged: **'Celebrate Life'**—a motto I inherited from my dad. No matter the situation, there are always reasons and ways to celebrate life each day. This became the foundation upon which my brand took shape. **BE YOU #celebratelife**

Even today, I may not have all the answers related to my brand and a clear roadmap of where I want to take it. But I know I have a solid foundation to stand on as I prepare to take the flight further. Yes, I dreamed Big. Without a clear vision of the future, I carried my dream of creating a brand for over a decade before taking the first step towards its realization. Now, I know the value of dreaming big.

I could have easily stayed in my secretarial position for life, within my bubble of comfort. Handling backstage tasks and supporting others, I could have remained at the foot of my own mountain. But the peak of the mountain seemed too alluring and inviting. First, I had to climb the mountain of anxiety within me, steering myself on the path of self-discovery and knowledge-gathering. Gradually, I pursued my big dream.

That's my Super Power Number 1: Dream Big!!

And be prepared to develop yourself for bigger opportunities. You may ask, how do these opportunities come? When you diligently perform your everyday tasks while simultaneously developing yourself for new challenges, these opportunities come seeking you. Sometimes, they appear as crises your team faces, or as new projects or launches your company invests in. The opportunity might come disguised as a challenge that intimidates you, prompting a desire to retreat and say no. Should you say no? No.

My Super Power Number 2: Say yes and embrace opportunities with enthusiasm and positivity, no matter how frightened you feel inside. I learned this superpower early in my career, and it led to many opportunities that contributed to my personal and professional growth.

One such opportunity came rushing to me in the form of a mega product launch at Ramoji Studios in Hyderabad. This was when Ramoji was considered the Indian version of Disney World and the go-to location for major events. The event I had the chance to manage was massive, with the presence of the company's global management. From a junior secretary content with managing backend operations, I suddenly had to become the front face of the event, running the show on stage and addressing senior delegates alongside 350 participants. What a transformation that was! It gave me confidence about my own capabilities and also presented me in a new light in front of the senior management.

That one 'YES' opened doors to many more opportunities, and I began climbing each rock, fueled by my zest to achieve and reach the peak. The next opportunity that came knocking was even bigger moderating and managing the Organization of Pharmaceutical Producers of India (OPPI) Managing Director's Conclave, a significant networking platform attended by MD's from across India.

This event remains unforgettable for many reasons, one of which was me being naive about soft skills and grooming etiquette at that time. I was overdressed, looking more suited for a wedding than a professional event. Though I carried myself with confidence, I couldn't help but cry when I got home. Yet, as various situations often do, this situation also brought valuable lessons. That day, I decided to completely transform myself.

My Super Power Number 3: Work on yourself to enhance your personality inside out. You may be getting management, marketing and other industry specific pieces of training. But soft skills and grooming are equally important in a corporate setup. Enhancing your personality gives you unsaid confidence and sets you up to face anyone or any challenge as well.

The senior leadership in our company was getting trained by great image consultants and I took advantage of this opportunity for my own development. I would reach the training earlier than everyone for setting up the training and ask queries to these trainers and in return gain insights that have helped me greatly in my journey of transformation.

Why are soft skills so important? Well, let me tell you about a funny incident I had to go through. Table etiquette is one of the major and most visible parts of soft skills. Owing to my great contribution to some Out of Box Projects and a CSR event, I got an opportunity to have breakfast with our Managing Director at the Taj. These moments with the MD were earned through my hard work and commitment. We drove in his best-of-the-class Mercedes to the Taj. He definitely left me in awe of his charismatic and chivalrous personality.

It was time to eat breakfast. He took a nice, crisp dosa and sat down to eat it in style with a fork and knife. This was simply impossible for me. I never imagined eating a dosa with a fork. Of course, you want to present the best side of yourself. So, what did I have for breakfast at the Taj? Two glasses of orange juice. That was the only thing I could manage without making a mess. The occasion itself was significant. I absolutely loved the interaction with the MD, but to this day, I laugh at myself and those two glasses of orange juice.

These simple yet highly effective superpowers I learned and implemented in my daily life have provided me with great motivation and strength to rise and perform in my career. The process of learning and self-improvement continues. Today, my confidence stands at a completely different level. My dad's lesson—'Celebrate life no matter what'—helps me celebrate every small win along the journey and find peace with every failure that teaches me a lesson.

What have these Super Powers finally taught me? One simple thing – **Everything we need is right there within us. All we have to do is believe in ourselves. Keep learning. Keep growing.**

My Brand: Dream coming true...

"The right partner will not complete you. You are already whole. The right partner will expand you. They will catalyze your growth and elevate your consciousness."

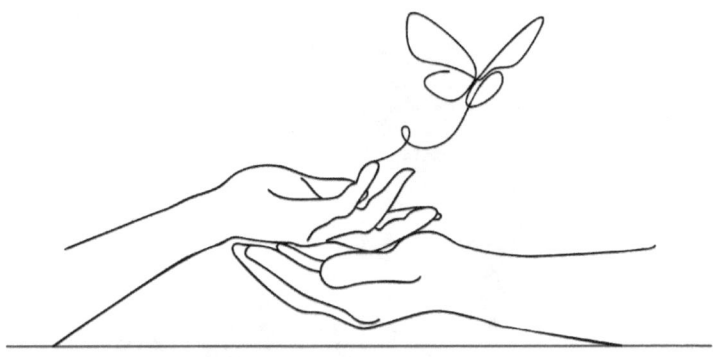

CHAPTER 7

AN UNCONDITIONAL SUPPORT

We, women, are fortunate to be a part of an age filled with opportunities and empowerment. Societies all over the world are becoming more and more aware of Gender Diversity, Inclusion and Equality.

Today, as organizations worldwide endorse the idea of gender equality by promoting and providing equal opportunities to women, we need to look deeper—or rather, at the root level—what about our families?

It is rightly said, "Women will have true equality when men share the responsibility of bringing up the next generation." Any significant societal change needs to start with individuals and families. Only when a woman finds unconditional support from her family can she embrace the opportunities with a free and happier mind. Without that understanding, compromise would be the way out. But, why compromise? Be it opportunities or family, why choose? Women can have it all when the men share the responsibilities on equal terms.

I am happy that I could witness the advantage of this simple philosophy. "Family isn't an important thing. It's everything." This quote from Michael J. Fox applies to a selfless man I met and fell in love with three decades ago. Generally, it is said that behind every successful man is a supportive wife. Well, it applies the other way around as well. Behind every successful wife is a supportive husband. I am extremely proud that my life partner has always considered both of us as equal partners in the family who share both opportunities and responsibilities.

Marriage is not just a union of two individuals, but the coming together of two families. I am truly blessed to be embraced by a family that is grounded, humble, and deeply believes in the strength of unity. Their warmth, understanding, and encouragement have given me the freedom to pursue my dreams, for which I am deeply grateful. Our marriage, beautifully consecrated at Tirupati with the blessings of Lord Venkateswara, bridges two distinct worlds—Gujarat and Andhra Pradesh. Coming from a close-knit Iyengar nuclear family to a vibrant Gujarati joint family, I initially wondered how to adjust to such a new dynamic. However, every step of the journey has felt effortless, as each family member welcomed me with open arms and hearts full of love.

And my ever supportive spouse made the journey of our marriage more comfortable and meaningful. It is easy to say, "I am a family man." But to be a family man, you need to commit a lot. You must put yourself at the back and keep your family always first. Then, neither your career nor your progress can hamper your commitment to your family. My hubby has always been this selfless man who will not think twice whenever the family needs him. He is not his priority at all. He will never say no and goes out of his way to provide the required time and support without expecting anything in return.

He always knew about my aspiration to do more and grow in my career. Right from day one, he has been a strong pillar who has encouraged me to take up new projects and say yes to new opportunities. He would simply say, "If I can dream and pursue my dream, why should you not? You go ahead and I will take care of everything." These words weren't merely uttered by him, but he has made them come true through his actions.

Without stable support, working parents can face significant challenges. It is often observed that a woman's career takes a setback in such situations. But having a partner like mine is a blessing for me and the entire family. We have shared responsibility for everything. When he had a travel plan, I would manage and pay all necessary attention, and I'm proud to say he has done the same, if not more. Owing to my job, even today, I travel a lot and sometimes stay away for weeks. Yet, I can focus on my work knowing that my better half will happily take care of all the responsibilities. Yes, happiness is the word you can't miss in this sentence. Whatever he does for his family, he is absolutely happy about it.

Once, due to an emergency, one of us had to be home for an extended period. We discussed possible solutions, and the next thing I remember is my husband resigning from his job. Right at the peak of his career, he chose to resign to take care of his family. It was a big compromise on his part, but he simply said, "When my family needs me, I should be there." This incident still leaves me and my daughter in awe, and I continue admiring him for his dedication as a family man.

Though we are busy working parents, I am beyond grateful that we have together been able to inculcate the right values in our daughter, thanks to the support we have given each other. A responsible, dedicated father is equally important as a mother.

He is the one who has given me strong wings to fly. Anytime I felt dispirited, he always raised my spirits, saying, "Don't crib. Look at your journey. You have done wonderfully well looking from where you started your career." His words and robust support have always been my anchor in my difficult times.

As an individual, he is incredibly easy-going and connects well with almost everyone he meets. He can seamlessly join any conversation in any crowd. What sets him apart is his remarkable ability to make people laugh, with a style of humor that is innocent and non-offensive. When he's around, laughter is contagious.

I recall a time when we invited his boss and family over for dinner. I had put a lot of effort into preparing the meal, but just before we sat down, our daughter and the boss's child insisted on having pizza. This sparked a lively debate. He quietly observed the situation and then intervened, saying, "No problem, we will have pizza. And, as usual, we will feed the homemade food to the cow tomorrow morning." Our guests stared at him, and I shot him a puzzled look. He continued innocently, "Yes, we do this every time. We make sure not to include onion and garlic in our food because the cow doesn't eat those, you know." Moments later, his innocent comment led to uproarious laughter, and we all joined in. To this day, it remains a topic of conversation whenever we meet them, and they teasingly ask, "Do you still feed your cow?"

Another incident showcased his simplicity and innocence. One of our neighbors is a fashion designer who creates pieces for major design houses in Mumbai, including the celebrity fashion house of Manish Malhotra. While visiting them, during a conversation, our neighbor mentioned, "Although this is a three-bedroom apartment, one of our rooms is filled with wardrobes full of orders for MM." In an innocent moment, my husband, unaware of popularly used acronyms for fashion celebrities, exclaimed, "MM... MM Mithaiwala?" Everyone exchanged puzzled looks before bursting into laughter. My dear husband then had to be informed that MM was Manish Malhotra and not the famous Mumbai's Sweet Shop – MM Mithaiwala.

His humor keeps our home vibrant and our relationships with friends and family lively. He has a unique talent for brightening any situation, never allowing anyone to stay sad for long when he is around. He always finds ways to bring happiness to others and is a sought-after person for help. People seek him out, and he is consistently available, often going out of his way to help others. Sometimes, he doesn't even consider how tired or busy he is; one call for help, and he is there. I suppose he has never learned to say 'NO.'

The unconditional love and support, considerate and helpful nature, and innocent humor are just a few of the wonderful qualities of this perfect family man. This kind of unwavering support is essential for women to truly recognize their potential and unlock the best versions of their lives and careers.

I have continuously witnessed changes happening in organizations for two decades. I often hear these words, "Hiring and promoting talented women is the right thing to do for society - and it's an economic imperative." Many organizations are working with this motto and creating many opportunities for women. While organizations are adapting to these healthy transformations, I think our societies and especially families also need to evolve for women to embrace these opportunities.

And when I say families, I don't just mean husbands; fathers, brothers, and other women in the family also need to realize the importance of support.

TRUE EQUALITY = Equal Opportunities + Equal Responsibility.

With my lifeline, my spouse - Sameer

My in-laws : a beautiful tight-knit family

My Father and Mother-in-law

With my Father-in-law

My Father-in-law (an excellent artist) with his painting of Shrinathji

The musketeers of the family

"The importance of good people in our life is just like the importance of heartbeats. It's not visible but silently supports our life."

CHAPTER 8

HOW PEOPLE SHAPE YOU

*I*n the corporate world, as you climb the ladder of positions, people management becomes the key role in your career. In popular terms it is called 'People Handling Skills'. I would like to call it 'People Understanding Skills'. Whether it is the senior management, peers & colleagues or junior executives, understanding them with clarity and being able to drive projects successfully in association with them, keeping everyone contented and engaged can be an overwhelming responsibility. And that is the challenge I enjoy the most.

People are the backbone of any organization. It is the people who create organizations. It is people who create families, communities, societies and nations. People shape people. At every point in time, you are learning something from someone and someone else is learning something from you. "Everyone you will ever meet knows something you don't." - Bill Nye. Hence, people are the prime capital of life. Be ready to learn and the mentor appears. Be prepared to learn from your interaction with people and you will find people of great value.

I am glad to have many mentors in life, including my parents, teachers, bosses, colleagues, juniors, friends, my partner, my daughter, and many more. I am even more glad to have an open mind and be a sponge to grasp something valuable from every interaction with all these people.

My colleagues and friends often ask me, "How do you manage every one with so much empathy and understanding?" This quality has been engraved in me right from my childhood days. My parents always taught me to be very courteous and humble above everything else. My dad would treat people like postmen, sweepers, cylinder delivery persons, and other helpers with great care and warmth. He would offer them a seat and give them water and snacks. He would speak to them politely and make them feel good. My little self was continuously observing the warmth and love he was offering to these unknown people. These early childhood memories have shaped me. Growing up in such a home has taught me the importance of treating people just like how you would want to be treated. This has helped me greatly as an individual and also as a team leader by being empathetic with my teams rather than demanding and commanding. "Management is about persuading people to do things they do not want to do, while leadership is about inspiring people to do things they never thought they could." - Steve Jobs.

Excellence starts with listening with empathy, building trust, and showing respect. By being proactive and offering honest yet kind feedback, we create an environment where people feel empowered to take initiative. When we support and believe in one another, we unlock the potential for greatness in everything we do.

Owing to successfully delivering on the additional projects at the organization, I was nominated for a 2-year Neuro Leadership

Coaching Program conducted by International Coach Federation (ICF). The program itself was quite interesting, and what intrigued me more was understanding the science of the brain, of handling emotions of ourselves and others. This fascinating science kept me glued to the program.

During this program, I was assigned a personal, master coach – Dr. Colleen Lightbody. Our one-on-one sessions were extremely deep, empowering, and enriching. Initially, I believed that a coach was supposed to have all the answers and help solve life's problems instantly. However, this program and my interactions with Colleen made me realize that a coach is a normal human being with a remarkable ability to listen and ask powerful questions that make you think deeply about everything.

I distinctly recall the specific session in which we delved into one aspect of my life that was hindering me from moving forward. It was obstructing my ability to make clear decisions and take even the simplest actions. I felt trapped, and despite my best efforts, I couldn't uncover the answer I sought. The coach remained immensely calm with me during that session and kept pushing me to seek the answer. I cried my heart out for some time and then became quiet. Amid the crying, pushing, and quietness, I finally found the deepest obstacle in my life with one powerful question from the coach. That moment will remain etched forever in my memory.

Finding that one obstacle brought in such clarity that I started seeing everything in a new light. It brought a drastic difference to my inner world. It changed the way I took decisions and actions. To the outer world, I might have looked the same, but within my consciousness, a permanent shift had taken place. No more obstacles could obstruct me in the journey of my life. My coach played a passive but vital role in that session. Her listening, questioning, pushing, empathy and understanding were all so empowering in that moment. My journey from weakness to finding the biggest strength within me was so beautifully facilitated by her.

"A coach doesn't show you how to do everything. They unleash your mindset so that you can decide." I thank my coach for helping and guiding me to shift my thought process completely. I also owe her my newfound interest - Coaching. The program of 2 years made me interested in the subject so much that I became keen on pursuing it as my second career. Becoming a coach, I aim to create a difference in people's lives just the way my coach did so for me. It takes a great effort to put yourself in other's shoes and navigate them to find their own answers.

I have been interested in people. Listening is one of my best characteristics. People always need a listener, and I am always interested in lending my ear without a hint of judgement. My keen interest in people made me pursue an Management Course in Human Resources during the earlier part of my career. I got the opportunity to do fieldwork through my organization. Fieldwork is a valuable resource for learning and enabling oneself to contribute productively based on those learnings. I had the opportunity to meet many doctors, retailers, and distributors—all key players in the business process. Each one provided valuable insights and information, which I absorbed thoroughly, later analyzing and delivering the best solutions for the betterment of the team and business. Experiences like these help navigate tough situations in professional life.

I vividly remember one workshop which we conducted in a village called Biharganj near Patna. The rural salesforce along with Doctors had flocked in dressed as if they were attending a wedding but with great enthusiasm to gain some new learning. For them, a big organization was hosting the workshop and each one of them looked forward to learning. The village had only two hours of electricity daily at uncertain times. Surprisingly, none of them cribbed about the heat, or the mess due to the power cut but participated in huge numbers and overwhelming attitude.

Their attitude and keenness were humbling reminders that the desire for knowledge and improvement can transcend any circumstance or environment. Their enthusiasm was infectious, and it made me reflect on the importance of maintaining a lifelong curiosity and openness to learning.

As I continue on my path, I carry with me the spirit of those eager learners, constantly seeking to absorb new insights and apply them in meaningful ways. It's this shared journey of learning and growth that connects us all, reminding us of the potential within each of us to make a difference in the world.

People are like walking books. Interacting with them are amazing chapters leaving key lessons that shape you. Among the many people who have shaped me, I tried to celebrate my coach in this chapter.

Truly people matter a lot. "It's not what you have in life but who we have in our life that matters."

"*Daughters are a promise that love will live on.*"

CHAPTER 9

THE PHOENIX WITHIN

*W*hen a daughter is born, the mother is the happiest as she knows she is holding a mini version of herself and a lifelong friend. As I write this, I am pulled into a tide of memories—memories of her. My daughter. My heart, my reflection, my teacher, all wrapped in one.

Life may have given me many valuable lessons through my people, places, books, and experiences. She has empowered me with golden nuggets of wisdom. Right from the moment she took that first breath within me, I have been a witness to the soul with a relentless fighting spirit and never-give-up attitude. From my little bundle of joy to becoming my Best Friend Forever, I have learned key lessons of life from my daughter.

From the very beginning, she was *something else*. Not just strong, but bold in a way that left no room for hesitation. Her laughter has been contagious, filling every room she entered, and her spirit— oh, her spirit— like a fire.

But, as life is, it tested her at every juncture. And it tested us as a family. It was during her 10th Board Exams. She had studied and prepared for the exams extremely hard. Three days before the exams, she stepped out to freshen herself up and take some photocopies. At the shop, she slipped and twisted her leg. The pain was terrible. On visiting the doctor, we realised it was a ligament tear and her leg needed to be plastered. She was supposed to keep her leg stable at an angle. No movement at all. The excruciating pain, being stuck in a wheelchair, and the tension of being able to attend board exams together was a great challenging condition. The condition itself was very hard to endure, not just physically but emotionally as well. The kind of pain inside and outside that no parent can shield their child from.

As an adult and a parent, I could only give her words of hope and of course the required treatment and support. I wished I could wave a magic wand to erase the pain inside her. I felt inadequate as a mother to solace my daughter.

We approached the school and the board to seek permission for her to write her exams in a wheelchair. She had to keep her leg elevated on a table in front of her while writing her papers. Thankfully, she was granted permission. Despite the agonizing pain and uncomfortable seating, she managed to complete her exams back-to-back. And, oh dear! Did she pass? Voila! She did it with flying colors, scoring 96.5%! We were extremely happy and proud of her.

Two years later, she fell again, injuring the same leg in the same spot. Her initial fall had weakened her leg, making it prone to similar injuries. She has injured the same leg five times, each occurrence coinciding with a milestone event in her life. The doctors treating her were perplexed and took all the case papers to create a case study for aspiring medical students.

Every time her leg was injured it meant restriction of movement for few months. She would miss out on a lot of things mainly, going out, meeting friends, attending college and classes. It affected her overall health and well-being. Inspite of these challenging times, she cleared her exams with outstanding results each and every time.

As a parent, we can go to extremes to protect, to motivate, to provide opportunities, to support our children. Yet, there is a limit. No matter how much we do, there is something out of our reach. Your child's inner world cannot be controlled by you. The feelings, emotions, and thoughts are ungoverned and can be most tricky, especially through adolescence.

When I was feeling small and helpless, I saw her rise like a phoenix! Shining in the glory of her determination and the go-getter spirit. There were days when I could see the struggle in her eyes, and the pain was obvious, but each time she fell, she got up—stronger. She shook it all off and gathered herself to write a better story of her life. Being resilient.

She became my reminder that life's challenges don't have to break you. They could, instead, shape you into something stronger, something better. "Fall seven times, stand up eight." is a Japanese proverb I only read. She exemplified it as a living reality through all her struggles. All the adversities couldn't keep her from shining brighter and brighter. She kept her chirpiness alive within her, keeping our home vibrant and joyful. She stayed amazingly positive and kept us positive as well. "Everything is fine," she would always say.

She excelled academically—outshining expectations and earning scholarships, accolades that reflected not just intelligence but hard-won grit. In college, she embraced leadership, becoming the President of the marketing cell—a role that perfectly suited her natural ability to lead, inspire, and rally others. I watched her in awe, remembering the little girl who once questioned her place in the world. Now, she was commanding rooms, building bridges, and creating change.

Besides acing her academics, she dived into all sorts of fun activities—strumming the guitar, making waves in swimming, zooming to various dance styles, cracking abacus levels, and much more! She didn't just try them; she nailed them. Her streak continued in college, where she grabbed the Star Performer award.

And then there were her friendships. I remember how, at one point, she was uncertain of finding true friends. And yet, somehow, not only did she find them, but she became an anchor for those around her. She offered comfort, wisdom, and unwavering support. How amazing it was to watch her sort things out in her friends' lives, and I would wonder when my little girl grew this big. But I always knew her logical, practical and sorted mindset is what makes her the advisor in her friends' group and in our family as well.

I love how incredibly passionate she is about people and life as well. She has always been grateful for all she has and willing to share the good stuff with the underprivileged. I remember our visit to an Orphanage in Goregaon. The experience made her look at life's privileges with gratitude and created a sense of responsibility and sharing in her. She insisted on sharing the best of her toys with the kids in the orphanage. I am glad she took that key lesson from the humble environment and people she met there.

This is what makes her special. She is always ready to learn, imbibe and also live the lessons learnt. Her knack and urge for learning inspire me to a great extent. I have been watching proudly every single day as she did little things to keep herself and the family cheerful, lively and happy always.

She taught me something so valuable. Through every setback and every obstacle, she found a way to turn it into an opportunity. To turn it into something positive. In a way, she became my guide. Often, I found myself seeking her advice, asking, "What would you do?" And she always had a unique way of seeing things clearly, of making sense of the chaos. It was as though her wisdom came from a deeper place, a place of experience and strength that I couldn't help but admire. And as she is currently away from me making her career, I miss getting that perspective of hers that made everything feel so easy.

I want to tell her, - You are incredibly brave, and your courage and resilience continue to inspire me every day. No matter what challenges life throws your way, stay strong and stay positive. To me, you are a true champion. As Maya Angelou beautifully said, 'We may encounter many defeats, but we must not be defeated.' You have embodied this truth every step of the way, and I have no doubt you will carry it with you always. I am so deeply honored to be your mother, and I am beyond proud of the person you've become.

Our story—one of love, resilience, and an unbreakable bond—is a story I wouldn't change for anything

With the light of our life, our daughter - Priyal

★ **TAKE A BREAK** ★

Find the words in the box below.

```
B A D A G R A T I T U D E M
L P R E S P T Y S G D E M A
R T R E F L E C T I O N B D
O A E A F A R B A O C A R E
L K S S A A G L A N E M A E
A R I W A C I A V S S A C O
C E L E B R A T E L I F E F
O S I C A E A A H S M A O R
L P E A O A A A E A P Y P I
L E N L A T A B A A L J P E
A C C L B I I F A L E T O N
B T E Y A V I B F O J M R D
O Y S U O I H A E C O I T S
R O H P T A G K A Y S U H
A U A P T Y A A A R S A N I
T R I A L E A D E R S H I P
I S U P P O R T L A A A T A
O E A E S H A P N P K A I A
N L A D A P T A P R A I E A
A F A A A A Y A J N U S A
```

HAPPY	GRATITUDE	COLLABORATION	FRIENDSHIP
CELEBRATE LIFE	ADAPT	VIBES	CREATIVITY
RESPECT YOURSELF	SIMPLE JOYS	REFLECTION	RESILIENCE
EMBRACE OPPORTUNITIES	LEADERSHIP	SUPPORT	FAITH

"There are those who give with joy, and that joy is their reward."

— **Khalil Gibran**

CHAPTER 10

THE JOY OF GIVING

A friend at work introduced me to this orphanage, which I visit with my family at every memorable event. I have created countless cherished memories with the kids here which have taught me the real meaning of life, humility and happiness.

I vividly recall my first visit here. I engaged with the children, gaining insight into their daily routines, activities, interests, and perspectives. One girl shared with us the area where she stored her clothing. My thoughts halted as my gaze got glued to that small space with a maximum of 4 pairs of clothes. Just out of curiosity and wit, I asked her, "Ohh.. you have so much. Can you give me one pair?" And she immediately responded, "Of course you can! Take whichever you like. This is more than enough for me." In fact, she added she would be happy to give.

This girl having just 4 pairs of clothes, without wasting a second to think, was happily ready to give one to me. Her generosity and selflessness were a profound lesson, teaching me that true wealth is not measured by what we have, but by what we are willing to share with others. This moment was a turning point in my understanding of giving and gratitude. That's when I learnt what giving truly is. To happily give what is yours, without holding a thought of belonging.

Living in a life of luxury with wardrobes full of fancy clothes and yet filling our carts with the latest trends, we keep attaching ourselves to every piece we own. We create a sense of belonging with everything we buy and bring into our lives. And then we make it so difficult for ourselves to depart from these materialistic things. Why?

The interaction with the girl made me aware of myself and my thoughts about life and happiness. For months, I couldn't buy a single piece of new clothing reminiscing on how little we can easily live with. Generally, we give donations from our affluence after we have spent on our necessities. And she was ready to give from whatever little she had. Yet she was more happy in giving. It made me realize the joy of giving is not in the material value but in the act itself, in the willingness to offer what little you have to make someone else happy.

I read this somewhere, "The joy of giving lasts longer than the joy of receiving." I feel it also is a purer joy to experience. To receive a gift is a great feeling, but it is short-lived. Till the time we have opened the wrapper, seen the gift, used it once or twice. That's it. Whereas when you give, you experience a more deep-rooted happiness. The happiness that stays with you for a long time and paves a path to contentment.

Here is an illustrated story of when I felt this intrinsic happiness of giving.

The Joy Of Giving

Only by giving are you able to receive more than you have and also more than you give.

Another time, I remember, I was walking into a cake shop to buy pastry for my daughter. A little boy approached me, "Can you buy me a cake? It is my brother's birthday." For a few moments, I looked at him suspiciously. But then in Mumbaiya style he pinched his throat and started pledging, "Maa Kasam.. maa kasam.." And something unexplainable happened within my mind at that moment. "For how many people do you want the cake?" Six was his reply.

I went inside the cake shop and bought 6 different pastries for him. On seeing me walking out with a box for him, his joy knew no bounds. He was laughing and crying at the same time. In a spurt, he started dancing throwing his hands in the air. "Yehh.. Balle.. Balle.." He rushed with the box back to his gang and showed it to a boy who I guess was his brother. The brother looked beyond him towards me and smiled wide. Believe me, I was smiling wider with teary eyes. The joy I was feeling within was immeasurable and immensely satisfying.

I reached home and told the entire incident to my daughter. She replied, "So cute. You could have given these pastries as well." Listening to this made me even happier. I felt so nice to have passed on some good values to her.

Well, buying six pastries was not a very big thing for me. But that joy of giving and seeing the joy in the boy's eyes was a big thing. It reminded me that the smallest acts of kindness can go a long way and have a heartfelt impact on both the receiver and the giver. Moments like these are treasures in life that light up our journey with warmth and compassion. They teach us that true happiness is found in sharing more than acquiring.

Such experiences have instilled in me a deep appreciation for the simplicity of giving, reinforcing the belief that generosity is a powerful force that can transform hearts and lives. It is these acts of kindness, however small, that ripple outwards, creating waves of positivity and hope in the world.

These are a few of many encounters that have guided me to cherish the joy of giving, a value I hold close to my heart. It serves as a constant reminder that true wealth lies not in our possessions but in the love and kindness we extend to others. Tiny acts of kindness can unleash massive waves of happiness!

The joy of celebrating life's little moments

"Stay close to people who feel like sunshine. People called as friends."

CHAPTER 11

FRIENDSHIPS AS I KNOW IT

I was asked last week, who is your best friend?

I don't know…

I don't use that language anymore. It doesn't fit. I have friends who hold the keys to different doors of my personality.

Some open my heart. Some my laughter. Some my mischief. Some my sin. Some my civic urgency. Some my history. Some my rawest confusion and vulnerability. Some friends may not be the closest to me, but they hold the most important key at a particular moment in my life. Others, who may be as close as my skin, might not have what I need today.

And that's okay. It's perfectly fine if our friends don't hold every key. How could they? It isn't a failure if they don't unlock every door of who you are. The million-room mansion of identity cannot align perfectly with anyone.

Reflecting on friendship, I'm reminded of a wild adventure I took with two women. They met for the first time on this trip through me - Talk about a recipe for an unforgettable adventure. So, three women from different walks of life, one car and a three day road trip to Goa. What could possibly go wrong?

Well, it all started when I saw that the Times Women's Drive was headed to Goa, my dream destination for a roadtrip. Two of my bucket list dreams in one go? Count me in! I love driving, and the idea of cruising to Goa with some soulful tunes had me grinning from ear to ear like a kid in a candy store. But... the butterflies in my stomach were having a party.

Of course, the Times Women's Drive wasn't just about looking cute behind the wheel. I needed two partners who could drive, calculate, be active on social media, and have fun. Simple, right? Spoiler: It wasn't. After some serious soul-searching and a few cups of coffee, I roped in *Bubbles* and *Buttercup* (yes, Powerpuff Girls were involved in the naming process). With their help, and some not-so-subtle Facebook prodding, we got enough votes to join the challenge!

The orientation party was like a scene out of a high school drama—everyone else had been friends for ages, and then there was us. The awkward trio. *Great,* I thought, *we're going to be the ones eating snacks in the corner.* But then Bubbles, ever the social butterfly, dragged me over to snap a few group photos with our car number placards. The result? Pure chaos, lots of giggles, and some seriously questionable poses. We bonded faster than I could say "road trip."

The theme that year was *Cancer Awareness for Women*, and we decided to call ourselves the "*Knockout Queens*" because, well, every woman is a queen, and we could totally knock out breast cancer with a little awareness. We designed some killer graphics and came up with the genius idea of matching pink outfits. Because, why not? Pink pants, pink tees—basically, we looked like a girl band on a budget.

Now, about those graphics: The vendor I entrusted to apply them returned my car with nothing but printed boards. Nothing was stuck on the car. *Fantastic!* I thought, *this is how we start.* But with a can-do attitude and a lot of tape, we set to work in the dim light of dawn, turning our car into a "Knockout Queens" billboard. It was chaotic, but we laughed our way through it—and that's when I realized that the *journey* really was what mattered.

With the car looking—let's say—*adequately* ready, we hit the road. The sun was out, music blasting, and I was already having too much fun to think about winning. Bubbles took on the role of our official "timekeeper," calculating all sorts of things with the seriousness of an accountant, while Buttercup kept us well-stocked with snacks (because driving without snacks is basically a crime).

Of course, as with all road trips, we had our fair share of tense moments. There was that one time my car stalled in a Ghat area, with a truck behind us and no escape in sight. But Bubbles? Cool as a cucumber. She hopped in, waved the truck driver to stop, and took the wheel. The truck driver might have been impatient, but Bubbles handled it like a boss. Later, we almost collided with a BMW, but Bubbles' quick reflexes saved us. Buttercup? She was in the back, doing her best to keep us calm with a hug and some well-timed "You've got this" pep talks. Later, the BMW driver came over to thank us for our quick thinking. She was genuinely grateful. *I should have asked for a tip,* but I didn't want to push my luck.

At some point, we realized we'd been so focused on calculations, we'd missed the beauty of the road. We decided to put the map away, stop the constant timing, and just enjoy the ride. And enjoy it we did—chatting about everything from family dramas to work rants to bizarre childhood stories. It was a far better use of our time than any prize could have been.

One of the highlights of the trip was Ganpatipule. The evening aarti at the Ganpati temple by the sea was the most peaceful, calming moment of the whole adventure. It felt like the universe was reminding us that sometimes, the journey is about the people you're with, not just the places you go. And being there with Bubbles and Buttercup made it all the more special.

Due to some political upheaval in Konkan next day, the competition was canceled and we took a scenic route to Goa. No stress, no deadlines—just three women having the time of their lives. We even handed out small mirrors with breast cancer awareness messages, because *spreading the love* is always in style.

By the time we reached Goa, we weren't just participants—we were a team. A team that had laughed, argued, and grown closer with every mile. The final party was way fancier than we ever expected, but Buttercup urged us to celebrate our journey, regardless of the glitz and glamour. So, we did. We dressed up, showed up, and celebrated the memories we had created.

This trip taught me that friendship doesn't always come in neat packages. Sometimes, it starts with a shared goal and a willingness to step outside your comfort zone. The real reward wasn't the destination—it was the conversations, the laughs, and the bonds formed in the most unexpected of circumstances.

And in the end, I learned a valuable lesson: The best friendships are often the ones you don't see coming—like a surprise pit stop, right when you need it the most.

I am truly blessed to have many such incredible friends who have been my pillars through every season of life. Though we may not talk every day or share coffee as often as we'd like, there's an unspoken understanding that no matter the time or the circumstance, I can always count on them. I am deeply grateful to God for gifting me with friends whose presence in my life feels like a gentle, comforting sunshine—always there, warming my heart, no matter what.

With Bubbles and Buttercup and the 'Knockout Queens' car

"Work life integration comes when you stop chasing balance and start embracing the flow of life, where work and personal time both nourish your spirit."

CHAPTER 12

WORK-LIFE INTEGRATION

"*I* don't believe in work-life balance. I believe in work-life integration. Make your work and life meaningful and fulfilling, and they will complement each other." This quote by Ratan Tata, inspires me.

Work-Life Balance is not something you find or you create but integrate by doing what you love. I am convinced by this thought. Balance is not readily available out there. No matter how many books you read or training you attend or follow your coaches to the tee, you need to work upon integrating life and work.

Integration is about blending work and life in a way that fuels both personal fulfillment and professional success. It's not about dividing time, but about finding alignment—where our work energizes us and our personal life enriches our work.

One of the crucial obstacles to integration is Perfection. Many might not agree with my perspective, but I learned this valuable lesson during many incidences in my professional journey.

Right at the start of my career as an Executive Assistant, I put in my best effort to make life easy and perfect for my boss. But after work, when I would ask myself, 'Am I feeling happy?' The answer would be blurred and packaged in the satisfaction that at least my boss wasn't complaining.

It is my honest contemplation that perfection is good, but we miss out on a lot of things. For instance, at one point in time, I had ten pending tasks in a day. But being obsessed with doing things perfectly, like making the excel sheet look beautifully perfect, I could complete a maximum of only four to five tasks on that day.

The excel looked amazing, but I wasn't lauded for that effort. On the other hand, I was judged harshly for the pending tasks. A less beautiful-looking excel sheet would have given me the opportunity to complete the pending tasks.

Over time, I've come to realize that embracing imperfection doesn't mean compromising on quality or giving up on excellence. In both my personal and professional life, I've found that when I let go of the need to be perfect, a world of possibilities opened in front of me. I become more present and more appreciative of the moments that truly matter. This shift in perspective has helped me cultivate a more fulfilling and integrated life, where success is not measured by flawless execution but by meaningful experiences and genuine happiness.

On practical grounds, in the pursuit of perfection, timelines get missed. And many a time, in the ever-running corporate world, the timelines are most crucial. The win is not in perfecting the small nitty gritty but in delivering the end goal within the deadline.

I was part of a 9-month-long cross-function collaborative project with multiple project heads working together to deliver a digital functioning system, which was critical for the organization. There were too many trajectories and a rigorous follow-up was needed to stick to the timelines. We focused on crafting a beautifully and perfectly functioning system but missed important timelines and it made us unsure of getting enough budget to complete the building of the system.

During this project, I witnessed people raising questions about me being the team lead. Also, each one wanted their share of appreciation. It took a great deal of time and effort on my side to deliver up to the expectations and keep the team intact, where each one felt appreciated. At that point, I diligently made my work the priority, which meant my home and family had to take a back seat.

This is where I would say "We need to make choices and relish those choices based on our circumstances." I made a conscious choice of keeping work above home during that project. Making that choice and sticking to it was the vital element that helped us deliver on the promises we made as a team.

You need to have the capability to stretch. I worked during the day, night, weekends, all occasions, festivals, and everywhere and every time in those months. But there are three more crucial factors that I would like to add here.

Number One: An unconditionally supportive family. I am blessed to have a family that understands and applauds my efforts at my workplace. I guess it requires an equal understanding from all the members of the family. I have equally championed each one's choices and goals. What you sow, so shall you reap. I get the support I need at all times for which I am always grateful.

Number Two: Acceptance that each day is not the same. The choice moves from one priority to another. Not every time work is a priority. Depending on the circumstance, you need to be flexible in deciding your priorities. Some days, we need to push our limits to achieve our goals. However, it's equally important to recognise when to pause and recalibrate.

The true strength lies in our ability to adapt according to the situation. Some days, work takes the front seat and some other times our family makes the work sit on the back seat. "If we want to live a wholehearted life, we have to become intentional."

A very close relative was in hospital in a critical condition. Being unconscious for 10 days, the situation needed the entire family's attention. At the same time, I got nominated by the office to go to Paris as a team lead. It was a dream opportunity, huge pride and a rare chance. At a crucial juncture like this, I had to make a choice. And I chose family. I knew, and I had accepted that you cannot attain it all. Life is more important than success.

Though I chose family, I had to ensure my team's deliverables were met and they were able to travel. I worked through my stay at the hospital, home and all the tension as well. My team helped me amazingly through the difficult times, and we could complete our requisite deliverables.

Also, I guess God answers the prayers of those who put in their best effort. A miracle happened, and everything came back to normal with my relative getting better. And yes, thanks to my family's support, I was able to travel to Paris and live that dream opportunity.

Number Three: is a well-managed team. A good team helps you attain the professional goals. Just like a family. Even if one person in the team is negative or dismissive, the whole team is thrown out of the equation. And again I would say, I have been blessed to work with great teams who have supported my work-life integration beautifully.

Putting all these thoughts together, I realize I have missed out on one major principle. Being present. Wherever you are, be there 100%. Physically, mentally, emotionally, spiritually.

This has been a root of creating more meaningful relationships be it family or work. With a demanding work profile, I may not be able to spend a lot of time with my family and friends. But when I am with them, I ensure I give my 100% attention. It might be just for few minutes or few hours.

Giving 100% attention even for few minutes is far more valuable compared to spending 24 hours with a distracted mind. I have witnessed the power of focused awareness in the simplest of activities like cooking. At times, I may add a lot of things to a dish, but with a distracted mind, it never becomes a delicacy. Whereas, when made with complete awareness, a simple cup of tea tastes better than most delicacies and gives happiness to the soul.

I read this somewhere - "Your greatest contribution in life is not your work. Your greatest contribution is showing up and being fully present in the lives of people you are surrounded with." And this basic fundamental has helped me achieve work-life integration. Making the right choice, sticking by it, being present, having a supportive family and work teams and accepting that not every situation is the same are my foundations of WORK-LIFE INTEGRATION.

"Open your mind to possibilities. We live in an infinite universe where everything is possible."

CHAPTER 13
SPIRITUALITY IS A STRENGTH

*I*magine building a house of cards, each piece carefully placed to create a delicate balance. One wrong move, one slight nudge, can send the entire structure tumbling down. Similarly, a situation comes when how one small mistake can lead to a mammoth disaster, shattering everything you are made of.

It's astonishing how a seemingly insignificant error can set off a chain reaction, leading to consequences far beyond what anyone could have anticipated. Like a single domino toppling the rest, one oversight can unravel the fabric of what seemed like a perfectly woven life.

I went for a usual dental treatment – a root canal. The procedure, which I had hoped would alleviate my discomfort, instead led to unexpected complications. The anaesthesia that I was given was supposed to be worn out after a few hours. But that small overdose led to a rare and worst complication ever. My mouth just couldn't open beyond 1 mm. On follow-up, it was detected to be a rare condition and I was informed that my mouth might open but it would take few months. There was no specific medication or treatment available for it, but it will heal on its own without a defined timeline.

Can you imagine your mouth unable to open beyond 1 mm? That meant a complete halt to my life. I had to switch to a liquid diet. The long talks were no longer possible as I had a lot of discomfort while speaking. Working in this condition was nearly impossible. At times, while speaking, I used to actually mumble and this frightened me to a point it could impact my voice. This was frustrating and isolating.

The critical factor was the root canal that was done on the wisdom tooth which is connected by a joint to the jaw, bone and muscle. And the jaw lock resulted in it all getting locked up.

What followed this dramatic unfortunate incident? No one was keen to take up the case spoilt by another doctor. I incessantly googled the topic and everything around it.

Then, a very senior dentist, Dr. Murli Motwani, through our friend's recommendation took up this weird case. I am truly grateful to Dr. Motwani who accepted the challenge of treating a case that was complicated and, frankly, in disarray. At every step of the way, there was not only expert care but also constant motivation and reassurance. What stood out most was his remarkable humility. His kindness and dedication made each visit feel like a step towards not just recovery, but a positive, uplifting experience. His unwavering support turned what could have been a daunting process into something I looked forward to. It's individuals like him, with their compassion and skill, who make the world a better place.

During the treatment, I was suggested to take physiotherapy for my mouth. That was another weird thing to experience. Just like you use a jack to change a car's tyre, my mouth would be opened with a jack. Then using various mouth props like wooden spatula sticks or bite blocks, the physiotherapy would be done. After months of this crazy physiotherapy, a little but no remarkable improvement could be seen.

We also consulted many senior dental surgeons recommended by Dr. Motwani. The solution was to get operated. It meant breaking the jaw open. I was told that it would be a long operation and a lengthy procedure of rehabilitation which would take months post the operation. But the way it all sounded, it meant nothing would be normal again. I couldn't find the confidence to decide to get operated. And what an outrageous response I got from the surgeons, "No amount of blessings and prayers will help you beyond an operation."

All this while, work continued with its usual projects and deadlines. The deliverables were always met, losing my speech during presentations was one of my biggest fears. But I learnt to keep smiling through it all. I couldn't share the story of my pain at work always. Despite all the difficulties and losing mental peace, I tried to stay positive and focus on the small victories. Slowly, I learned to adapt to this new way of living. Support from friends and family became my lifeline, offering encouragement and understanding. I also discovered a new found appreciation for simple pleasures, like the warmth of a smile or the comfort of a friendly presence. People around me ensured that every day I get a proper diet through soft pureed and yet tasty preparations.

Keeping myself absorbed in work and life, I took the big decision of not operating. I also stopped the physiotherapy for sometime. I surrendered all my pain, difficulties and fear to my faith and my beliefs. Deep down, I held onto the conviction that just as everything got locked in one moment, there would come a day when things would feel normal again.

One day I felt a strong calling to visit Shirdi. Upon discussing with my spouse, we decided to go visit. We went to the temple and took darshan in the morning. On returning home, while brushing my teeth at night, which was another weird thing as I had to brush my teeth with a baby brush inserted in my finger and push it in my mouth, I heard a crackling sound from that side of the jaw which was locked. I wondered what happened and one more fear crept into me.

From that night, I heard a regular crackling sound while brushing every day. That one moment, that one sound, every day, I realized that my mouth was opening little by little. And a few months later, everything came back to normal all by itself. Believe me, if someone asks me about that condition, I would like to forget it like a tormenting nightmare that bothered me for more than a year.

Deciding not to operate and stopping all treatment had a leap of faith behind it. I came to believe that I could go through the pain and that there always was a light at the end of the tunnel. Everything will be fine one day. I said to myself, "The pain I am enduring is not more than the strength I have been blessed with. It is a challenging time but I know - This too shall pass."

I am not sure what was the reason behind my relief. Whether it was the visit to Shirdi, prayers of my family and friends or the medical support and motivation from Dr. Murli Motwani or it was the time for my pain to be erased. The strength I found during the hard times will now stay with me forever. My spirituality found a new meaning and new reinforcement.

The journey taught me that sometimes, surrendering to faith and embracing the unknown can lead to unexpected resilience and inner peace. With each passing day, I grew more confident in my ability to face whatever lay ahead. I learned that while the future may be uncertain, the present moment is always within reach, offering an opportunity to find peace and purpose.

In embracing this mindset, I discovered that the light at the end of the tunnel was not a distant destination, but a reflection of the light within me, guiding me forward with hope and unwavering faith.

Physio session with Dr. Murli Motwani

A dental clinic full of positive vibes and happiness with Dr. Murli Motwani & Dr. Sneha Motwani

"The world is a book and those who do not travel read only one page."

CHAPTER 14
WONDERS OF TRAVELLING

I am going to start this chapter with the most memorable travel experience of my lifetime—**PARIS!** A dream destination. I was assigned to lead Team India for a Champions meet in Paris. We were a group of 32 Indians, and I was leading them with pride. It was a rare opportunity that came with great responsibility. I vividly remember the surge of emotions as I held the Indian Tricolour Flag and loudly cheered, "India… India!" It was a glorious moment, representing my country in a foreign land, leaving a permanent mark on my heart.

Following the meeting, I reminisce about my most cherished visit to the Eiffel Tower. Reaching the top of the marvellous Eiffel Tower, I was thrilled to recollect my journey of life. "How far I've come to become a team leader and reach here," I thought. That breathtaking experience remains fresh in my memory, as if it happened yesterday, and I will cherish it forever.

Travel is often hailed as one of the most enriching experiences life has to offer. Whether you're exploring a new city, diving into a different culture, or simply escaping the daily grind, the beauty of travel is its ability to transform you. It engages your senses, emotions, and mind, creating moments of wonder and deep connection.

Discovering New Cultures

Travel exposes you to new customs and ways of life. It's an eye-opening experience and creates a deep respect for the world community as a whole. During my travel to Maldives, for example, I was struck by the importance of respect and politeness—small gestures like bowing or sharing tea had deep cultural significance. It reminded me how much culture shapes communication.

> *Experiencing new cultures nurtures empathy and broadens your understanding of human behaviour worldwide.*

Navigating Language Barriers

On a trip to Spain, we faced a funny situation owing to our limited vocabulary. My colleague mixed up speaking Spanish and accidentally ordered "chicken feet" instead of "chicken fillet." The waiter smiled and corrected us, and we shared a laugh over it. Language barriers can be funny, frustrating, and enlightening all at once. It was a reminder that language is not just about words, but it's about making connections and not stopping at your mistakes but enjoying them too.

> *The willingness to try and communicate in a foreign language can break down barriers and create lasting connections, while adding a bit of humour.*

Getting Lost, Finding Yourself

Once, I got completely lost while hiking in the Swiss Alps. It was one of my memorable travel experiences, but getting lost was stressful. Instead of panicking, I took a deep breath and embraced the moment. The solitude gave me time to reflect and appreciate the beauty around me. I eventually found my way back, feeling both exhausted and exhilarated.

> *Getting lost sometimes leads to the clearest insights. Life's unexpected detours offer fresh perspectives.*

The Kindness of Strangers

In Patna, on an official trip, I missed my bus to a remote village, Biharganj, and found myself stranded. A local man was kind enough to guide me to another bus—and even pay for my ticket. His kindness proved to me the universal nature of human compassion. It left a lasting impact on my mind.

> *Strangers often step in to help in ways that restore your faith in humanity.*

Learning Patience on the Road

In Australia, I missed a connecting flight due to a long security delay. Frustrated at first with the long wait and no updates from the airlines, I decided to make the best of it. I struck up conversations with fellow travellers and enjoyed a nice cup of coffee while adding a bit of humour. The delay turned into an unexpected opportunity to slow down and create meaningful connections.

> *Travel teaches you - patience, showing that sometimes the detours are where the real magic happens.*

Experiencing Nature's Power

I took a helicopter ride to see Mount Everest in Nepal where I witnessed nature's raw power. The ride among the huge snow-clad peaks with the wind howling and the snow flying around making the view disappear in a moment and get cleared in another moment was quite a wild experience. It reminded me how small we are in the grand scheme of the planet.

> *Nature has a way of grounding you, putting everything in perspective, and inspiring you to be more mindful of the planet.*

Embracing Simplicity

On a backpacking trip in Ganapatipule, I stayed in basic guesthouses with no luxuries, just a bed and a fan. With minimal distractions, I felt more connected to the local culture and myself. It taught me that happiness doesn't come from material comfort but from simplicity. This thought itself was quite liberating for me.

> *Travelling to places with few luxuries often reveals that we don't need much to feel fulfilled. It can help to reset our priorities and we can learn to appreciate the simpler things in life.*

Making Meaningful Connections

During a stay in a small village in Baku, I befriended a local woman who invited me into her home for a traditional meal. Despite the language barrier, we spent hours sharing stories and laughs. It was a reminder that some of the best travel moments are the unexpected, genuine connections we make.

> *Travel brings people from different walks of life together, and some of the most rewarding aspects of travelling come from the relationships you form—whether brief or lasting.*

Embracing the Unexpected

In Rajasthan, I planned a camel trek in the desert, but a sandstorm delayed everything. What seemed like a setback turned into a memorable evening spent with desert nomads, learning about their way of life and watching the sunset from a different vantage point.

> *Flexibility and an open mind can turn unplanned moments into the best travel memories.*

Along with meeting people and various life enriching experiences, the highlights of my travel also include the love for food and capturing sunsets & sunrises.

Food is at the heart of every culture, and one of the greatest joys of travel is tasting dishes that tell the story of a place. From a spicy curry in India to a fresh baguette in Paris or a sticky mango rice in Bangkok, each bite opens up a new world and lets you into the special story of that place. Sharing meals with locals or fellow travellers makes these moments even more delightful.

Sunsets and sunrises are reminders of the fleeting beauty in the world. Whether it's a golden dawn over a temple or a sunset on a tropical beach, these moments stop time, filling you with awe and leaving a lasting imprint on your heart.

Travel is more than just moving from place to place—it's about experiencing the world through new eyes, forming connections, overcoming challenges, and finding beauty in unexpected places. It's a journey that engages every part of you, leaving you changed for the better.

There are many more big and small experiences and learnings from travelling. All I would quote at the end is – "Wherever you go, go with all your heart."

"Rome wasn't built in a day, but they were laying bricks every hour."

CHAPTER 15

NO PAIN NO GAIN

*H*ave you ever dreamt of something that felt challenging, so far outside your comfort zone that it seemed almost impossible? For me, that dream was gaining an educational qualification from Harvard. Coming from a corporate background, where my days were consumed by deadlines, meetings, and targets, I never thought I'd have the time or the courage to pursue something so ambitious.

Being a lifelong learner, I would continuously google for various online courses. And I stumbled upon a leadership course offered by Harvard. A perfect match! As I read more about the program and its relevance to my career, something inside me stirred—a quiet voice telling me to try. I am habitual of reflecting on myself and the kind of leader I want to be, and this course felt like the perfect opportunity to transform myself.

I still remember the day I submitted my application. My hands trembled as I filled in the details, half-expecting rejection. The selection process was quite acute and extremely detailed. There was a 360-degree survey with an intense questionnaire and also included ratings on various parameters from peers, subordinates, seniors from the workplace and family as well. I was skeptical about how would these people assess me individually and professionally as well. But, later I was contended and felt proud as the amazing results showcased that people evaluated me excellently in all parameters.

Post the survey, there was an interview which again tested me well. Putting in my best effort was all that I had in my hand. Keeping my fingers crossed, I waited ardently for the final results.

And one day an email arrived from Harvard—a confirmation of my admission. It felt surreal. I sat staring at the screen overwhelmed by the realization that this far-fetched dream was now my reality.

I was too excited to embark upon this new journey of learning. We were a cohort of leaders from different companies based in different countries. It was quite an enriching experience being in touch with these professional peers and an excellent curriculum to work with continuously for the period of the course.

Amidst the course, one day, I received a phone call informing that my brother, along with my mother and his in-laws, had a major accident. His car crashed into a truck, resulting in serious injuries to all of them. I reached Bangalore, where they were admitted, immediately. And two days later, came the dreaded lockdown of 2020, when the world came to a standstill. The chaos and uncertainty challenged us to find new ways of working and living.

The regular patients whose treatments could wait were being sent back as space was to be made for the COVID patients. Overall, there was so much confusion around COVID, and the manpower was a bigger challenge. Nurses had to be running all around looking at COVID patients and also the serious patients like my family, who had to undergo operations. Around a month later, when they got discharged, we shifted to my brother's apartment. Ten people were staying in that apartment, including the four injured, my sister-in-law with her 3-month old, her sister, myself and the two help we hired for all the patients.

Space was already crunched, and the lockdown made it crazier with its restrictions and shortage of everything. It was so difficult to manage food supplies, cooking, cleaning, and getting medicines. Those 6 months were truly bizarre with us overcoming small to big challenges every day.

Amid all the challenges, I had to continue pursuing my course. It was an opportunity I had earned and simply couldn't ignore. I would carry my laptop to the hospital and sit in the waiting area, working on my assignments. And then would connect with my peers through the night for team discussions and projects. The peers were quite supportive knowing my family situation but I wasn't ready to escape through excuses. Also, diving deep into the course would alleviate my internal pain during that time. It kept my mind busy.

The course itself was rigorous, pushing me to think critically, collaborate virtually with diverse professionals, and redefine my understanding of leadership. It wasn't just about gaining knowledge; it was about discovering a version of myself which I didn't know existed.

I knew for sure that like most things in life, this isn't going to be completed without hard work and complete dedication. I am a staunch believer in "No Pain, No Gain." Life has taught me the same in its various chapters. Be it my first job, my Management

Course I did while working, or my role that grew from secretary to handling Human Resources to communications to digital, or the current profile of leading a South Asia team at a reputed company. I have always gained my share of achievement, accolades only after putting in tremendous and sincere efforts. And hard work has been a natural quality as I imbibed it from my parents.

During the course, we were required to tread through the assignments with a lot of teamwork. We were given several team projects to be completed. Each one needed to contribute and make the project valuable, functional and successful. Being in a different time zone than Harvard and most of my teammates, I had to work through the night. But each of us stretched a lot to listen to each other and learn from each other. I came across many case studies to understand how people from different countries and different organizations tread through their work.

As we created our group on LinkedIn to stay connected in terms of sharing and learning, I realized a different universe was being created. I always looked forward to any conversation in that group even after being exhausted.

And then came the day, when I got my certificate from Harvard on completing the course. Seeing the words Harvard and my name on the same glorious piece of paper was a moment of great pride! Believe me, I spent an enormous amount of money to frame the certificate in the most expensive frame bought from the best store in Mumbai.

Today, when I look back at that period, I'm reminded of how the most unexpected challenges can open doors to transformative opportunities. It was tough to manage all the personal challenges while keeping up with the demands of the course, but there is no shortcut to success. The Harvard experience didn't just give me a certificate; it gave me confidence, clarity, and a renewed sense of purpose. It taught me that dreams, no matter how impossible they seem, are always worth chasing. And what helps in a successful chase of your dreams is making the right amount of effort. At times, dreams like this ask you to stretch a bit too much and you should be ready to do so.

"No Pain, No Gain" is a phrase not just about sweating in a workout, but it's also true for mental, emotional, and even creative growth. The emotional and mental "pain" often leads to greater understanding, resilience, and success.

Remember, gains don't show up immediately! Think of it like planting a tree. At first, the seedling doesn't look like much, but with proper care and patience, you get a strong tree. Similarly, you may not see the results on day one, but one day, you will be lifting heavier weights or solving problems effortlessly!

Pain means Progress!! Think of your own brain as a muscle. Every time you tackle something difficult, you're essentially "tearing" old patterns of thinking and creating new connections. Every difficult conversation or challenging project is like a mental workout.

Embrace the pain and embrace the change! Pain is less of an obstacle and more of a signal that you're on the right track. It's like a *badge of honor* in the journey of self-improvement. Seeing my family going through such difficulty pained me a lot. But today it feels like all that has expanded my ability to handle challenges.

So, you see - "No Pain, No Gain" is a multifaceted philosophy that speaks to the value of effort, resilience, and the transformative power of discomfort. It's about embracing the struggle, knowing that it's leading you towards greater achievements—whether that's stronger muscles, a smarter mind, or a more resilient character.

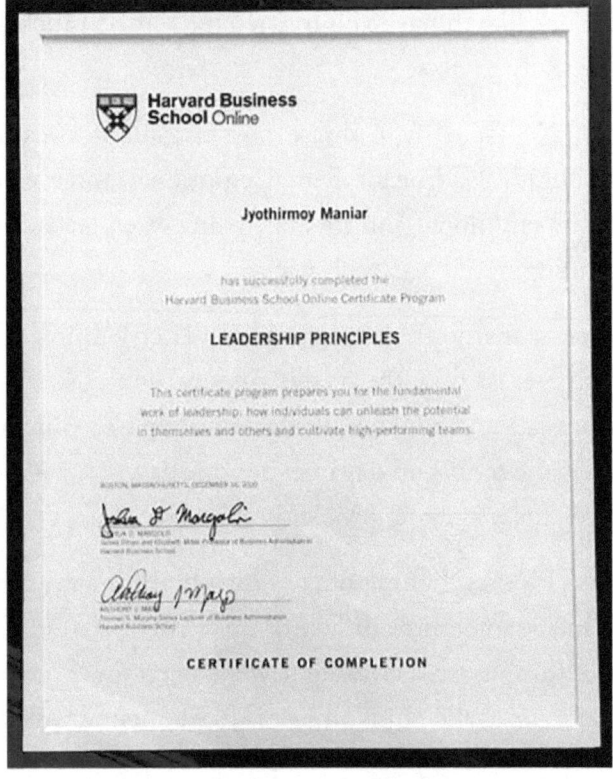

★ **TAKE A BREAK** ★

Decode the message below

|  S
  T
  O | H
  W
  A | I
  N
  E |

__ __ __ __ __ __ __ ,

__ __ __ __ __ __ __ .

"Happiness is not something ready-made. It comes from your own actions."

CHAPTER 16

NURTURING HAPPINESS

I was in Dubai for an official meeting. On the last day, one of our executives entered the room, overflowing with enthusiasm, showing his phone to everyone. When I inquired, with equal excitement, he eagerly showed me a video clip he was sharing. It was of his skydiving experience. He had planned and booked the skydiving adventure for himself before coming to Dubai—it was on his wish list. And here he was, standing in front of me with a beaming smile, radiating pure joy.

The video was not only beautiful but also quite thrilling. It was clear that the experience must have been breathtaking and incredible. The joy he felt combined with the surge of adrenaline was apparent from the way he recounted the entire story.

As I watched the video, a thought crossed my mind: "Wow! That looks amazing. Jyothi, if you could do this, it would feel like you were a superwoman flying in the sky. It would be like having a superpower!" But then I wondered, "Would I actually be able to do this? Can I really skydive?" I asked him several questions out of curiosity.

During the dinner that night, I discussed the same with our travel partner. He immediately began to persuade me. "Madam, do you want to do it? I'll take you there. Don't worry. People of all ages come and enjoy the experience. I'll go with you." With his persuasion, the video playing in my mind, and my own doubts and emotions, I found myself torn—"To do it, or not to do it?" I went back to my hotel room, still unsure, with the dilemma lingering in the back of my mind. After some time to relax, the thought of skydiving kept turning over in my mind.

Around midnight, I pulled up my laptop to check the skydiving bookings for the next day. It was a free day, and I had a late-night flight back to India. As I checked the booking section, I saw only two slots were vacant. "Should I book it? Should I not?" I was thoroughly confused. The cost was nearly 50,000 INR. "What if I can't do it after paying? What if something goes wrong? What would happen to my family?" As I pondered these thoughts, I saw one slot get booked, leaving only one remaining for the day. Finally, I told myself, "Forget it, Jyothi, this isn't your thing. Go to sleep." And with that, I went to bed.

The next morning, I rose at 4:30 AM, prepared myself, and headed to the skydiving location. The idea, by then, had completely grown on me. I contacted our travel partner, and we arrived at 6:30 AM, only to find the office still closed. We spent some time waiting at the nearby beach until it opened. While sitting there, I felt a rush of excitement, repeatedly telling myself, "I want to do this, I want to do this..." At that moment, my desire was strong, not just because of the video I had seen or to impress others, but for the sheer joy it would bring me. I went through a rollercoaster of emotions.

We went back to the office after it opened and I asked the lady on the counter for a slot. She replied with a sorry and told me further that all the slots were booked for the day. "You should have booked it online yesterday." I was on the verge of tears as I listened to her. "Why didn't I book it last night? I really want to do this…" I asked her, "Madam, I am flying back to India tonight. If you could please help me and get me one slot, I would be so grateful." I persuaded her like an eager, excited child. Seeing my persistence, she asked me to wait and told me that if any slots became available by noon due to cancellations, they would get back to me.

From 7 AM to noon, I was constantly moving around, observing the experiences of others. I witnessed a range of people, from young teenagers to senior couples, joyfully exiting with smiles on their faces. It felt as though they were truly savouring the moment. I found myself praying to God for what I desired that day—not to prove a point or seek adventure but for that sheer bliss… pure ecstasy!

My ears were tuned to hear the lady call my name. At 12:05, I finally heard her say, "Ms. Maniar." I couldn't believe it. The person with me shook me out of my disbelief and confirmed it was indeed my name. We rushed to the counter, where they told me a slot had opened up due to cancellations. However, since it was a last-minute booking, I had to pay an additional 10000 INR. Without thinking twice, I immediately booked it.

I was then taken through all the procedures of signing a few forms and instructions. I rushed through all of it. I just wanted to fly. I am not sure if it was madness or happiness at that point in time. Just then, the staff member asked, "What message would you like to leave for your family?" I paused for a moment and then said, "If I'm not there, the message my family should carry forward is to Live Life to the Fullest."

I admit I had butterflies fluttering in my stomach. But once I was out in the sky, it was the experience of a lifetime. How can I describe it? My heart was pounding, my mind was silent, my senses were on overdrive, and the roar of the wind was deafening. It felt like I was caught between a dream and reality, with the breathtaking sight of the world below me. Words fail to capture the feeling, but one thing is certain: you won't stop smiling once you've done it. You can't hide your happiness from the world.

To date, that experience lives on with me. I was so happy that I did it. I am thankful to myself for being courageous and listening only to my gut feeling that I want to do this... I want to do this... I did it purely for myself, my happiness, my feeling of ecstasy. I was being absolutely myself nurturing my own happiness. And that dive is always going to be the most cherished living memory of life.

Nurturing happiness by being yourself is about accepting who you are and creating space for your natural joy to unfold. It's not about forcing happiness or striving to meet some external standard of success but rather allowing yourself to feel content, grounded, and peaceful in your skin. Now this was a big one-time event which gave me that pure happiness. But then do we need to wait for such big events to create our happiness?

Happiness can be felt everywhere in all the little joys of life as well. That one big moment may be exclusive and scarce, but the little moments of care, being yourself and doing little things just for yourself can be numerous and enjoyed almost every day.

To give a few examples from my own life, I find happiness in -

- Listening to music especially when I am driving my car
- Rearranging my home, adding a little to my home now and then.
- Keeping little things of my identity in my workspace, making it like me
- Dressing up to my best to please myself
- Spending focused time with loved ones
- Finding little ways to make people feel valued
- And of course, whatever I do, I do it 'Dil se...'

Tandem Skydiving with Rua Brian

How can you Nurture Happiness by Being Yourself?

CHAPTER 17

A WRITER'S JOURNEY

Writing a book is a beautiful, exhausting, self-doubting, coffee-fueled adventure.

10% Writing, 90% Questioning Your Life Choices

Writing a book is mostly asking yourself, 'Why am I doing this?' about 100 times a day. At least once, you'll reach the part of your manuscript where you question every decision you've made in your life. 'Who am I? Why am I here? How do you even spell "narrative"?

The Writing Process is a Hot Mess!!

The writing process is basically this: Write. Think it's genius. Delete. Think you're terrible. Rewrite. Repeat. There is no clear line between 'genuine work' and 'binge-watching Netflix' and calling it research!

The Endless Editing Loop

Editing is like cleaning your house. You think you're done, but then you find more stuff that needs fixing. By the time you're done, you're wondering if you should've just left the house messy.

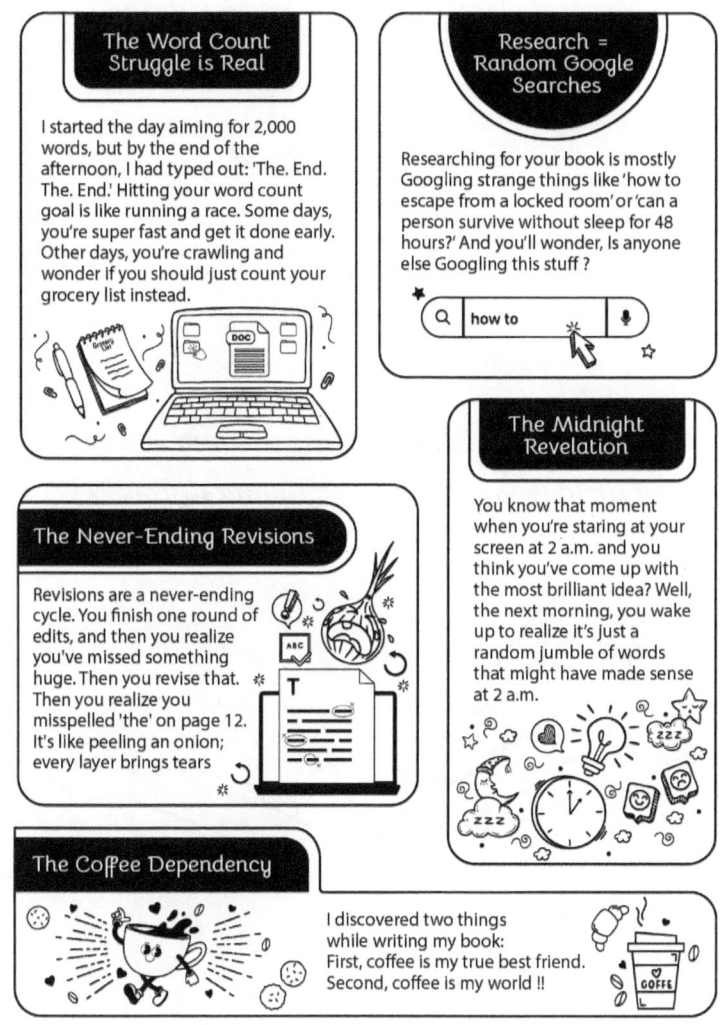

Writing a book is a marathon, a maze, and an emotional rollercoaster all in one. You go through joy, frustration, panic, and moments of brilliance. But in the end, when you hold that finished manuscript (or see it published), there's nothing quite like it. It's a personal triumph even if it feels like 99% chaos and 1% magic.

"Your true self is not something you find overnight; it's a lifelong journey of growth and discovery."

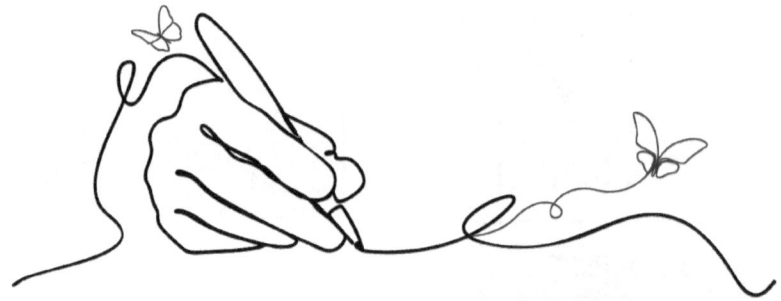

CHAPTER 18

A LETTER TO MY YOUNGER SELF

*I*t's been a while since I came across this quirky yet surprisingly insightful self-help exercise: writing a letter to my younger self. At first, I thought, "Why would anyone do that? Aren't we the same person? What would I possibly say?" But the more I read about it, the more I thought, "Okay, maybe I need to try this." And honestly, I'm not just doing this for me—I've got a hunch that someone else might find it just as eye-opening.

The toughest question I had to ask myself was: "Am I the adult my younger self would have wanted to meet?" And, oh boy, the answer was a bit of a shock. Not only is my current self very different from my past self, but I also realised that I might not quite be what my younger self had imagined. Naturally, I was tempted to give myself a hard time over it, but in the end, this whole exercise was worth it. And the lesson? "Just trust the process!"

Darling Jyo,

I can see we still share a love for the colour blue, and you're absolutely right—it's a perfect match for you and me. Every time I see your smile, I realise just how truly beautiful it is. Let that smile shine as often as possible because it reflects your heart and brightens the world around you. I am going to tell you a secret. You are going to be showered with compliments for your innocent and infectious smile all through.

You are still so young, with endless possibilities ahead of you. **Never lose faith** because your name, **Jyotirmoy**. It means "full of light" or "radiant." Embrace that radiance, for it will guide you even when the road seems uncertain.

Take care of your health. You may find yourself in a place where you're not "like the other girls," but remember, **you are never less than anyone else**. Movement, self-care, and a balanced lifestyle will bring you not just outer beauty but also an inner glow that will make you stand out. Later, you'll be grateful for the habits you build now. Trust me—**start now, and your future self will thank you!**

Your skin will face challenges, and acne will make you feel insecure. But remember: **it's not the end of the world**. It doesn't define you. **Don't let it steal your self-esteem**. Go to a dermatologist, take care of yourself, and know that your worth isn't tied to appearances. You are much more than skin deep.

In school, **you won't always be a topper**, and that's okay. You'll have your moments of brilliance, but even when you don't, remember: **doing your best is already a victory**. Your hard work will pay off in ways that matter more than grades. **Never let anyone tell you otherwise**.

Socialise more! **Expand your horizons**—meet new people, make lasting friendships, and nurture the relationships that truly uplift you. **Never force anything**; people who are meant to stay will stay.

And please, **always be kind**, especially when faced with challenges. Life is not a competition; it's a dance. Take a step back when you feel overwhelmed, breathe deeply, and remind yourself that **kindness is your greatest strength**. Every challenge is a lesson, and you will rise stronger from each one.

Don't be afraid to make mistakes, little one. **Forgive yourself**, learn from them, and move forward. Life is about growth, and no misstep will define you unless you let it.

You will face both scarcity and abundance. There would be times when you struggle to make ends meet and other times when you have more than enough. But here's the truth you'll come to understand: **money doesn't bring happiness**. However, some financial security will bring peace of mind, so learn about finance, build your emergency fund, diversify your income streams, and secure your future.

Choose the best, always. Whether it's healthcare, your education, or relationships, invest in quality over convenience. Don't compromise on your well-being or the things that truly matter. A little patience and research will save you so many headaches later.

Listen to your gut. **Red flags are there for a reason**—trust them. Be mindful, question what doesn't feel right, and always trust your instincts.

You will lose money, make mistakes, and sometimes feel foolish for it. But know that **it's all part of your growth**. You will learn, adapt, and move forward. It doesn't define your worth or intelligence—it's just part of the process.

Look your best, inside and out. Even when you're at home alone, take care of yourself. The way you treat yourself and your environment reflects how much you value yourself. **Self-respect is key**, and it begins with honouring yourself every single day.

When it comes to your career, **don't compare yourself to others**. Everyone has their own journey, and success is not a race. Focus on your milestones—celebrate your progress, no matter how small it may seem. **Your path is unique**, and every step forward, no matter how long it takes, is an accomplishment. Keep growing, keep learning, and remember: **your time will come**.

Turning 30, 40, or 50—these are not milestones to fear. **You will always be young at heart**, as long as you choose to be. Age is just a number, and your spirit will forever be vibrant.

Love yourself more than anyone else. You are worthy of the absolute best in life and **never settle for anything less** than what you deserve. Your dreams are valid, your goals are achievable, and you are capable of amazing things.

You're about to witness so many of your dreams coming to life. Just like this one right here—Writing Meraki! I can't even begin to express how deeply this journey has touched me. It's been such a gift to pour my heart and soul into these pages. This book is more than just words on paper; it's a reflection of passion, purpose, and the pure beauty of creating from the heart.

Remember, you are beautiful, inside and out. **You deserve all the happiness in the world.**

10 Points to Ponder Upon

1 Talk the Talk
Communicate clearly or risk becoming the person everyone nods at but doesn't understand.

2 Feel the Feels
Master emotional intelligence; it's basically like being a human mood ring.

3 Roll with the Punches
Adaptability is your superpower—change is the only constant, so might as well embrace it.

4 Time is Money
Manage your time like a boss. Procrastination is your worst enemy (and it's sneaky).

5 Think, Don't Just Google
Problem-solving: Use your brain, not just Google. Creativity goes a long way.

6 Team Player Vibes
Collaboration > Solo Mission. It's not about being a hero, it's about being part of the squad.

7 Conflict? Handle it Like a Pro
Disagreements happen. Handle them calmly, or be known as the office drama queen.

8 Stay Positive
A good attitude is like Wi-Fi. It makes everything better, even on the bad days.

9 Lead by Example
Leadership: It's not about bossing people around, it's about inspiring them to do the work and bring donuts.

10 Network Like You Mean It
Meet people. Make connections. You never know when you'll need a friend... or a coffee date.

Cover and Doodle Designs by
Manasi Khandpekar (Manache)
Email: manacheinc@gmail.com

In the journey of life, we cross paths with so many beautiful souls—both known and unknown. To those who have offered a smile, a kind word, or a helping hand, your warmth has touched my heart more than words can express. Each person, whether briefly or forever, has contributed to this tapestry of love, support, and joy.

To the ones who have shared their wisdom, their patience, and their love, I thank you from the bottom of my heart. Your presence in my life is a gift I will always cherish. And to the divine force that guides us, I am forever grateful for the kindness and grace that flow through every moment, every breath. May we continue to find beauty in every encounter and remember that gratitude is the light that that brightens even the darkest of days.

Gratitude turns what we have into enough, and transforms ordinary moments into extraordinary blessings…

Author welcomes your feedback..
You can reach out to Jyotirmoy Maniar at: Jyots99@gmail.com

www.ingramcontent.com/pod-product-compliance
Lightning Source LLC
LaVergne TN
LVHW041852070526
838199LV00045BB/1561